# Jealousy

## Get Rid Of Your Jealousy, Insecurity And Controlling Attitudes Within 30 Days

## For Men

## Francisco Bujan

### www.vitalcoaching.com

# Content

# Jealousy – For men - Coaching

Check this link:

## http://vitalcoaching.com/coaching.htm

# Jealousy – For men - Videos - Audios - PDF - ONLINE

Check this link:

**http://vitalcoaching.com/jealousyformen.htm**

# Part 1 – Jealousy dynamics

When dealing with unwanted jealousy, the first step is to understand why jealousy happens and why it can become obsessive.

In the next few pages, you will discover exactly why the human mind "devised" the jealousy response and why it can turn into a destructive spiral for your relationship.

# What dynamics are involved in taming your jealousy?

Jealousy can be one of the most destructive forces in a relationship.

Jealousy is originally a positive desire to protect your relationship.

It is an instinctual impulsion which aims at protecting the couple and the family.

Now, when you express jealousy, you are often achieving exactly the opposite of what you want.

You are attacking your partner's life and freedom.

Too often, this will achieve the exact opposite of what you want.

You express control and possessiveness and destroy the harmony of what you share with her.

Is this good?

Is this an expression of love?

If your jealousy is "justified" and there is a real threat on your relationship, then it is okay.

Jealousy is a weapon and you want to master that weapon.

It is a defense mechanism aimed at protecting what you share with your partner.

Now, imagine having a sword in your hands.

This is what jealousy is.

It is a psychic weapon you can use against what threats the stability of your couple.

However, this "jealousy sword" can turn against what you care for the most.

It can destroy the harmony of your relationship.

This means one thing: you want to master the skills and use jealousy in a wise way.

If jealousy is simply an emotional obsessive reaction you don't control, you are most likely to hurt those around you without a reason.

You don't want that, right?

In the next few pages, we will analyze the dynamics of jealousy and the way to tackle the unwanted obsessive aspect of it.

When you are obsessively jealous, it is not only your partner which gets hurt, it is you and the relationship as well.

In fact, it is a loss for everyone and everything involved.

It is purely destructive.

What you want is to master your reaction.

You want to use your sword wisely <u>only</u> when it is really needed.

The first step is to understand the dynamics involved.

Why does it exist in the first place?

The second step is to deal with obsessive jealousy and master your instinctual reaction.

# Unjustified jealousy is a misuse of your controlling power

Jealousy comes from a need to control your territory.

You consider that your partner is "your territory" and you want to be in charge of it.

Control comes from a need to secure your life and your environment.

It is purely instinctual.

Now, you can imagine that too much control can kill life.

Too much control annihilates freedom, space, love and harmony.

It creates a constricting mind set which stops movement, freedom, creativity, fun and excitement.

Control is a natural expression of power in your life.

When you are born, you are given a reserve of it.

The first use of your controlling power is on your own life.

Control gives you the ability to stay in charge of what is yours.

The keys that you have in your pocket are a symbol of this control.

They give you the power to open the door of your house and secure your personal space.

You use control to stay in charge of your existence.

You choose actions, attitudes, thoughts, emotions, belongings, beliefs, time frame, etc.

All these aspects of your existence are yours.

It is your birth right to own these aspects of your life.

As long as you apply control over what is yours, there is no conflict.

It is your right and it is a wise and healthy use of your controlling power.

Now, when you step into someone else's life and tell them what to do and when to do it, you are already stepping beyond the limits of your territory.

If someone steals from you your right to self determination, your whole spirit suffers.

You own your life and so does anyone else.

Your partner owns her life.

It is her birth right to decide for herself what she wants and when she wants it.

Now, when you partner with someone within a marriage or a committed relationship, you transfer part of your power to the relationship.

In fact, you accept someone else's authority and input into your life.

In other terms, part of your personal power is transferred to the couple's entity.

When you partner together, you join forces.

This is what your partner did the day she chose to have a relationship with you.

Now, what exactly was the agreement?

Did she say something like:

"From now on, you have control over my life. You can tell me what to do, when to do it and what to wear. I give you the keys of my being and you are now in charge"

Of course not!

This is not what she said.

The invisible agreement is much more along the line of:

"I stay master of my life and I partner with you to create a secure and harmonious relationship. I accept to consult with you when taking decisions and making choices simply to make sure that we are on the same wave length."

In fact, she never gave you the right to control her actions, time frame, beliefs or emotions.

All these still belong to her. It is still her birth right to stay master of them.

This means one thing:

When you use control to limit your partner's life, actions, attitudes or beliefs, you are already abusing your right.

You can't own someone else's life!

It is her birth right to stay in charge of her existence.

This is one of her most basic human rights:

Her right for self determination.

# Jealousy escalation and its destructive impact on your couple

Jealousy and control are dead end cycles.

The more you use it on your partner, the more your relationship dies.

You are killing what you were supposed to protect: the love between the two of you.

The moment you do abuse your power, you wake up in her the need to defend herself.

She starts feeling unsafe in her own space and needs to retreat deep inside to find resources of energy to go on.

<u>Obsessive jealousy is destructive</u>.

When you use it, you achieve exactly the opposite of what you want.

This is a dead end!

The moment you use obsessive jealousy against you partner, you create an emotional cycle and reaction which turns against what you love and care for the most.

You assume that control is okay when it is not.

You assume that to protect your relationship you need to limit your partner's space and freedom.

No way!

This is 100% an abuse of the original "relationship contract".

It is a deviation of the original agreement.

No one gave you the right to control someone else's life.

# Why jealousy is often the exact opposite to what you want

Go back to the original idea of jealousy.

The reason why nature created this instinctual response is to protect the relationship and family space.

Children and family need security.

Justified jealousy is your way of expressing a desire to protect your relationship's space.

Again, the original goal is to protect your relationship.

The goal is to protect love, harmony and freedom.

What you want is your partner to be empowered and fulfilled.

This is what your love expresses, right?

This is what you owe to each other when you join forces within a relationship.

You partner to empower each other.

You partner because you want the best for each other.

The moment you express obsessive jealousy, you work against these goals.

In fact you destroy part of your own dream.

You attack what you care for the most: your partner's joy and life satisfaction.

What is the solution?

The solution is to use your power in a different way.

Too much control kills life force.

You want to open your arms around your partner and give her space.

You want to replace the jealousy reaction by an empowering message of trust.

Imagine how this makes you feel.

Imagine what this brings in your relationship.

Control is a relationship killer.

Most couples who split run away from a feeling of limitation.

The relationship becomes too constricting and they need space.

It doesn't need to be that way.

The first reason to stay together is not because of control. It is because of love.

Love and trust are the solution.

You want to replace the obsessive jealousy reaction by these qualities.

In the next few pages, you will discover exactly how to manifest trust and shift the dynamics of obsessive jealousy.

# What works and what doesn't with tackling jealousy

When you try to shift an emotional reaction, you need a clear vision of what to do and why to do it.

The solution needs to match on many levels.

It needs to match your own individual plan, your partner's life and the plan for your relationship.

You need to tune into a model or a mind set which works better than the one you are using right now.

In fact, you want to evolve.

The good news is that there is a natural renewal power in you.

You already have the skills in you to empower your life and design a better instinctual reaction than the obsessive jealousy one.

Shifting an emotional reaction is about life mastery.

The door you open when you look at your life and decide to shift things around is the door of your mind.

You suddenly realize that you have the power to actually influence your emotions and your thoughts.

In fact, what happens in your mind is your territory.

This is the ultimate place where you can have an impact.

You have the power to redesign the way you react to emotional challenges in your relationship.

How do you shift your reaction?

You identify and train a new behavior and mind set.

Ideas, thoughts and emotions are mind "objects".

You can consciously design the way you stand in your relationship.

You can choose values, attitudes, beliefs and the qualities you want to manifest.

In fact, you are the designer of your life and relationship.

Now, transformation and change is not something which usually happens overnight!

Shifting a behavior requires understanding, focus and consistency.

However, when you realize the positive effects of a new refreshing mind set, you are most likely to adopt it instantaneously.

# Why tackling jealousy is a challenge

Simply trying to suppress an emotional reaction usually does not work.

What you need to do is <u>use your energy and power in a different way</u>.

Imagine a powerful mountain stream.

This is your power.

It is your energy.

Your emotional reactions are fed by this energy.

If you want to shift an emotional reaction, you need to adopt a new mind model.

Simply telling to this powerful mountain stream to stop is not enough.

You need to channel its energy in another way.

In other terms, you want to consciously build trust in your relationship.

You want to secure what you share with your partner and basically develop new communication skills within your relationship.

No worries, you won't kill the passion or the intensity.

The goal is not to delete the emotional power of your relationship.

It is to express it in a different way.

Suppose you see you partner building a friendship with one of her male friends.

The goal is to keep on communicating and sharing what is happening.

If she just had a phone call with him, and you feel challenged by that, you can go to her and say something like:

"You know what? I really don't like you talking to that guy. In fact, I don't want him to call here again!"

Now, what do you feel will be the effect of your words on her?

Destructive, right?

You will clash.

She will defend her right to see who she wants and when she wants to.

In fact you could end breaking up over this issue!

Is there another alternative?

Yes! There is!

Here is what you can say:

"So, how is he doing today? Still fancying you?"

Hey? What was that?

It is teasing.

You tease her with it.

You don't try to "swallow" what you feel.

You see this man.

He is a potential threat for your relationship.

You stay cool.

You know it is with you she shares her life.

You deal with it by teasing her about it.

You can as well say something like:

"He looks like a nice guy. You seem to have a good connection. Is he fun to work with?"

Dialogue, communication, sharing... These are magic words.

The moment you develop the ability to respond to this situation in that way, you open a whole new space in your relationship.

This is the space of trust!

It is empowering for the two of you and for your relationship!

Dare to try new behaviors and attitudes in situations like these.

You know that your mind and instincts have a whole range of possible patterns and attitudes you can manifest in your life.

Play a different card.

It does not mean that you stop playing.

You simply let go of systematically taking the possessive role and replace it with trust, respect, humor, etc.

These are attitudes you can train and develop right now.

# Why you want to do something about it before it is too late

With the previous example, you realize one thing: if you don't shift your behavior, this might lead to a break up.

You don't want to break up.

You love your partner.

The reason you got this book is because you know it is in your hands.

You can be respectful <u>and</u> still express your power.

You can be an empowering presence in your partner's life <u>and</u> still secure your relationship.

You want to do something about it because if you don't, you will probably lose what you care for the most.

Tensions in a relationship can't be stretched indefinitely.

At a certain moment, it breaks.

That's unless you find another alternative.

You, your partner and your relationship are worth it.

The key shifting factor is in you.

I know that the moment you decide to do something about it, it is within your range to shift attitudes and manifest a brain new level of power and trust in your relationship.

You are the designer of it!

It is in your hands!

Don't wait another minute!

<u>Make it your top priority for at least a month</u>.

Decide right now, that no matter how far you got, this is enough!

You want a new relationship equation and you want to develop a new mind set.

Obsessive jealousy is a drain for you, for your partner, your relationship and anyone who witnesses it.

# What does it take to shift a jealous attitude?

It is very simple:

It takes one to three months of focus and dedication to shift things around.

If you are ready, it even goes much faster.

Put it this way:

If you have been living with a mind set for 20 or 30 years, this mind set did create habits.

These habits are emotional channels, thoughts and beliefs associated with specific situations in life.

If you tend to overreact when you see your partner chatting with another man, you trained your mind to respond in a certain way in these situations.

Over the years, this created a mind set.

When you want to shift this mind set to an empowering feeling of love and trust, you need to retrain your emotional reaction in given situations.

You will be confronted with these challenges over a few months and develop a new way of reacting to these situations.

The goal is simple:

Create a win-win for everyone involved.

This means that there are no conflicts, draining fights or attacks on anyone's personal freedom.

Yes! It takes one to three months of focus to shift a mind set around.

You see yourself coming with new ideas and inspiration for your relationship.

You can wake up a whole new level of power in yourself and use it to protect what you care for.

You simply empower the way you stand in this.

# Jealousy triggers – Tackle them by making it VERY specific!

Certain situations or circumstances are especially challenging for the man who tends to be jealous.

It might be social events or the presence of her ex.

It might be long distance or the fact that she cheated before.

Later in the book I describe specific jealousy situations with the best strategies to solve them.

There is always a trigger!

The goal is to identify the exact situation in which you feel jealousy waking up.

Rather than saying:

"I am a jealous man and I don't know what to do about it!"

You say:

"I feel slightly challenged when I see her taking off to the gym and I know she will be seeing this personal trainer she is attracted to."

You just made it very specific!

Finding the exact strategy to a very specific jealousy trigger is much easier than fighting jealousy "in general".

This is why your first step is to define the exact situations in which you feel emotionally challenged.

Write them down!

You will recognize maybe 2 or 3 key situations where your jealousy or controlling attitude wakes up.

Your next step is to identify the best strategy to tackle that specific behavior.

# Jealousy outbreaks - How they are triggered by circumstances

Are there any elements or circumstances which can increase your susceptibility to jealousy?

Yes! There are!

In general, anything which lowers your level of personal power can stimulate jealousy outbursts!

Here are some examples:

- You face problems at work.
- You are physically sick.
- You face money problems.
- A relative just passed away.
- You are in a transition period, just decided to get married or moved to a new city or country.
- Etc.

Here is why these events can increase your susceptibility to jealousy:

Jealousy happens because your level of inner power is too low.

If you are fighting another battle or you are in a stressful period, your level of personal power and resistance to jealousy triggers can be lowered because your forces are already invested somewhere else.

When you are super confident and successful, you are less prone to jealousy.

Jealousy is a reflection of insecurity.

It is related with the desire to protect something which you feel is threatened.

Because your wife or girlfriend is so intimately part of your life, protecting your couple means protecting yourself.

Now, if your level of power decreases, you are simply more receptive to doubts, fears and emotional instability.

This is why you might tend to express jealousy in these specific circumstances.

Another set of circumstances which easily trigger jealousy is when you support her financially, you work for her or she works for you for instance.

When you support her financially, you tend to assume that you have more rights because of that. You can have a greater tendency to control her.

Somehow, you do expect a higher level of commitment because you give her money.

We'll check this situation in detail in another chapter.

What if she works for you?

Well, if she cheats, this threatens not only your love connection, it attacks as well your business or material stability.

You might express control not only as a love partner but as a boss as well!

This can stimulate jealousy patterns.

If you work for her, the same type of dynamics applies.

You depend on her not only for emotional or love life stability but for material stability as well.

If she cheats or leaves you for someone else, you might lose both a lover and a job!

This might make you more vulnerable emotionally or more prone to jealous attitudes.

# Male and female jealousy? Are they the same?

In theory, yes!

Jealousy in men and women aims at the same thing: trying to protect your relationship!

Now, the way women and men express it is actually quite different.

Guys tend to have the power to control a woman's life. When a guy gets jealous, he will tend to be emotionally abusive.

This emotional abuse dimension is a key difference.

A woman will express her jealousy more in the sense of emotional insecurity and turn this against herself.

Now, of course, you do have situations where women take an abusive position and control a man's life.

This happens especially if the woman is in a position of power and the guy tends to be soft.

In that case, emotional abuse and control will naturally happen.

You can as well have guys who are jealous but emotionally weak who turn jealousy into a self destructive pattern for themselves.

They express it as insecurity and you see them totally disempowered when they express their jealousy.

Remember that jealousy is always related with the desire to bring back a sense of security in your life.

It is related with the desire to protect the couple's unit.

When this couple unit is threatened, jealousy tends to wake up.

Now, if you are naturally very insecure in life, you will naturally wake up the jealousy pattern more often because you rely much more on your partner and couple for emotional security.

# What works best with jealousy issues? Coaching or therapy?

Let's first check what each approach does, ok?

Therapy originates in the medical profession and focuses on healing.

When you go to see a therapist, you believe that you need healing and that somehow, your present emotional reactions are dysfunctional.

Coaching originates in the sports and business field. It focuses on performance, success and life satisfaction.

You go to see a coach because you want more from life! The number one quality you get from coaching is extra power.

That said, if you are a jealous guy, what do you feel you need the most? Healing or extra power.

To tell you the truth, I think it's great you have the choice!

I know what I would choose myself, but of course my opinion is biased because I am a coach! Of course, I believe 100% in what I do because I see the results.

What about hypnotherapy? Well the results we seek are again the same, but the way to get there are quite different.

With coaching, my goal is to give you extra power and make sure that after a couple of sessions or going through the book and MP3 audios, you have all the tools and skills you need.

I like you to own the transformation process. I like you to be fully awake.

You don't need to be in an hypnotic trance state for this material to impact and make changes in your life.

I did explore the possibility of integrating a couple of hypnotherapy techniques in this material or in my coaching but consciously decided not to go that way.

Why? Not sure. It simply did not match with my approach energy wise.

Somehow I felt it was side tracking the core message I wanted to give you:

You are in charge!

You are in the control seat!

You own the transformation process!

It is extra power you need not healing!

The choice is yours really!

# Part 2 – 10 strategies to deal with obsessive jealousy

# 10 strategies to deal with obsessive jealousy

Here is a summary of your 10 steps with some extra tips.

When it comes to unwanted or obsessive jealousy, the final challenge is about using your emotions is a different way.

If you know your jealousy is unjustified and you want to shift it to something more positive, you have to retrain your instinctual reaction.

The goal is simple: replace the jealousy emotion by an empowering feeling of trust.

The key question is:

How to retrain an instinctual response?

Here are some key steps you can take:

- The first step is to understand the dynamics involved - Originally, Jealousy is an instinctual response aimed at protecting a relationship.

  This is the first goal of your instinctual response. However, when you express obsessive jealousy, you are achieving exactly the opposite. You are destroying your relationship. Excessive possessiveness is a relationship killer.

- Stop finding excuses - The reason you express obsessive jealousy is because a part of you justifies it. You find superficial excuses and imaginary threats to be over possessive.

  Don't hide yourself. You know what you are doing and you know it is wrong.

If you can't measure to other men, do something about it - Get yourself new skills, develop a new look, remove what is unattractive in you. Work on your personality and personal power.

Get validation from other women - The reason you become possessive is because you feel your self worth depends on your partner's exclusive attention.

The moment you get some of this from other women (female friends, light flirts, etc) you feel empowered and valued.

Get help! - Sometimes, the only thing you need is a second opinion to make you open your eyes. Have a few sessions with a coach or a therapist.

Do this alone or with your partner. A close friend's opinion might do the trick as well.

Redefine cheating - Chatting with one of her male friends is not cheating. A light flirt is not cheating. Cheating is not a fantasy, it is an action.

You can't control someone's thoughts. The real limit has to do with exclusivity in sex and other aspects of intimacy. Is she crossing the line or not?

Face your fears - If you believe she is way out of line if she goes partying on Saturday night, go with her one time and check it out. You might realize that your imagination does play tricks on you.

Confront your beliefs with real facts. Don't use vague feelings as a justification for possessiveness.

Work on it together - Sometimes you strengthen the jealousy pattern in each other. You get jealous and possessive. She reflects this pattern and limits your space as well.

If this is the case, work on it together and tackle the negative pattern in both of you at the same time.

Focus on trust - Trust is the real alternative to jealousy. When possessiveness is gone, it is replaced by an empowering feeling of trust. Wake up this quality in your relationship and choose to trust your partner whenever you can.

Do it for yourself first - Being obsessively jealous is energy consuming for you. It is a waste of your precious time. You are the one who will first benefit from a healthier mind set. You deserve it. Your partner will naturally be empowered by it.

You will realize one simple thing: the moment you do take these steps, you will already manifest new levels of mutual trust in your relationship.

It takes some time and dedication to give your emotions a new program.

Consistency is the key.

This shift won't happen overnight. Give yourself the target to solve 90% of this issue within 1 to 3 months.

Make it your top priority at least for the first month.

Use your will power, determination and whatever you need to break through.

Invest yourself in it.

The moment you set your mind into empowering your relationship, you invoke new refreshing forces in the core of what you share with your partner.

Take action! You and your relationship are worth it!

# Positive jealousy is originally aimed at protecting your couple

Originally, Jealousy is an instinctual response aimed at protecting a relationship.

This is the first goal of your jealousy instinctual response.

However, when you express obsessive jealousy, you are achieving exactly the opposite.

You are destroying your relationship.

Excessive possessiveness is a relationship killer.

There is no way around this.

You must know that when you use control on your partner, you kill her joy and pleasure to be alive.

You destroy your partner's life.

At the end, she will wish you never got together and even never met.

She will run away and never come back.

You must know this and repeat it to yourself over and over again until you decide to shift your attitude.

If you don't, consider this your last warning.

I am giving it to you in her name and in the name of your relationship.

Abusing your partner's freedom is not okay!

It will never be!

Your role in her life is to protect her space and freedom; not to use your power against her.

# Stop finding excuses

The reason you express obsessive jealousy is because a part of you justifies it.

You find superficial excuses and imaginary threats to be over possessive.

Don't hide yourself.

You know what you are doing and you know it is wrong.

There is a common belief amongst men, women and couples that when you are in a relationship, you have to give away your life to your partner.

This idea is old fashioned and goes 100% against the human spirit.

The human spirit is and wants to stay free!

Distance yourself from old fashioned macho attitudes.

You can express your power and be a fully dignified male without having to control a woman's life to feel that way!

You can't own another person's life!

So, don't try to justify obsessive jealousy in the name of protecting your relationship.

There is no excuse for obsessive jealousy.

# If you can't measure to other males, do something about it

Get yourself new skills.

Develop a new look.

Remove what is unattractive in you.

Work on your personality and personal power.

Your present limits are not your real limits.

If you feel insecure about your talents and skills, take action and develop them.

Society is competitive.

There is no doubt about it!

You want to play fair.

If you feel you miss the "competitive edge" in the love and dating scene, develop new skills.

Hoping that your partner will stay with you because you limit her space is a big mistake!

It might rather lead to the end of what you share with her.

If you want to enjoy long lasting love and an exciting partnership, make sure you pick up some of your personal challenges and keep evolving and developing yourself.

Here are the main areas in which you can get new skills:

- Business
- Career
- Self growth
- Health and body
- Social life
- Spiritual development
- Relationship skills

- Etc.

The possibilities are infinite; so play the game and play it fair.

If you believe that what you have to offer does not measure, take steps to develop what is missing.

This will give you the extra confidence kick you are looking for.

# Get validation from other women

The reason you become possessive is because you feel your self worth depends on your partner's exclusive attention.

The moment you get some of this from other women (female friends, light flirts, etc) you become less desperate and feel more valued.

What your partner gives you is love and validation.

Now, the moment you realize you can get these from other sources, it empowers the way you stand in your relationship.

It is okay to have a light flirt.

It is okay to sometimes fantasize about other women.

It is okay to loosen up slightly the boundaries of your relationship and realize that there is a world out there.

Obsessive jealousy can be the result of isolation.

You isolate yourself and the relationship within a cocoon of energies.

What you want now is open up and connect.

Your partner stays number 1.

Being in a committed relationship must not stop you from interacting with the opposite sex.

# Get targeted help!

Sometimes, the only thing you need is a second opinion to make you open your eyes.

Have a few sessions with a coach or a therapist.

Do this alone or with your partner.

A close friend's opinion might do the trick as well.

There is no shame in getting some targeted help or support with that.

In fact, it is one of the most empowering steps you can take.

No need to reinvent the wheel!

Many men have been where you are right now.

Why not use their experience?

There is a world of knowledge and expertise you can tap into.

If you feel challenging to train a new behavior by yourself, be wise and connect with a fresh source of support and inspiration.

No need to take the role of a victim or therapy patient.

This is not what it is.

You are healthy and perfectly functional.

Now, what you want is simply to gain extra power and new skills.

You want to discover new ways of handling a given challenge in life.

Look around you.

Be discriminative and do connect with sources of empowering support which can help you take your life to the next level.

# What EXACTLY is cheating?

Chatting with one of her male friend's is not cheating.

A light flirt is not cheating.

Cheating is not a fantasy, it is an action.

You can't control someone else's thoughts.

The real limit has to do with exclusivity in sex and other intimacy aspects.

Is she crossing the line or not?

Cheating is a very specific action.

It involves intimacy.

Now, if you react because your wife did cheat on you, it is probably justified, right?

What are the facts?

Who does she share her life with?

Is it with you or with a men she saw once at a party?

You did catch a glimpse of excitement in her eyes?

There is nothing wrong with that!

Your partner can receive validation from other men without this being a real threat on your relationship.

In fact it is empowering for your couple.

Put it this way:

Even though she has the choice, it is still with you she decides to be.

You win! She wins!

# Face your fears

If you believe she is way out of line when she goes partying on Saturday night, go with her one time and check it out.

You might realize that your imagination does play tricks on you.

Confront your beliefs with <u>real facts</u>.

Don't use vague feelings as a justification for possessiveness.

<u>Real facts!</u>

<u>Most obsessive jealousy is based on delusion</u>.

It comes from envisioning events, feelings and thoughts which do not exist.

It is a delusion.

Can there be a real threat?

Yes! Of course!

No need to play dumb either.

You can stay awake and aware but measure with exactitude the <u>real</u> extent of a threat on your relationship.

Step away from vague feelings and confront yourself with <u>real facts</u>.

If you have doubts, take steps and check them out.

# Work on it together

Sometimes you strengthen the jealousy pattern in each other.

You get jealous and possessive.

She reflects this pattern and limits your space as well.

If this is the case, work on it together and tackle the negative pattern in both of you at the same time.

Dialogue, trust, love and partnership are qualities you invite consciously in your relationship.

These are the nectar of what you share.

They are the core values of your relationship.

The best way to solve tensions is with dialogue and diplomacy.

Your relationship is an ever evolving organism.

When you reach the limits of what you can do together, there is always a next possible step.

This often involves gaining new relationship skills.

Long term relationship success is about inviting change and renewal in your partnership.

Dare to look beyond the limits of what you already know.

It is a vast topic and there is another book available on the topic of relationship empowerment.

Check the relationship section on vitalcoaching.com for more on that.

# Focus on trust

Trust is the real alternative to jealousy.

When possessiveness is gone, it is replaced by an empowering feeling of trust.

Wake up this quality in your relationship and choose to trust your partner whenever you can.

Trust means that you open space in your partner's life rather than limiting her.

You give her power, energy and validation as a human being.

Trust is one of the key foundation qualities in your relationship.

It is one you can invite and consciously develop by choosing for it whenever you can.

Trust empowers your relationship.

Tell her you trust her.

This creates a unifying bond between the two of you.

# Do it for yourself first

Being obsessively jealous is energy consuming for you.

It is a waste of your precious time.

You are the one who will first benefit from a healthier mind set.

You deserve it.

Your partner will naturally be empowered by it.

The moment you decide to shift a negative pattern in you, you empower your life straight away.

In fact, it gives you an immense feeling of victory and satisfaction.

You are the first one who wins from it.

You shift your emotional base and stop wasting your time trying to control something you can't control.

All this energy which was used for fighting and worrying is now free.

You can reinvest it in various ways in your life and relationship.

This is about gaining long term life mastery.

Mastering an unwanted jealousy reaction is one of these tests you face in life.

Now, the moment you understand how this works, you open a door to new possibilities.

This is about your mind!

This is about your life and the satisfaction you gain from it!

Realize that you are the architect!

You are the designer of your existence!

# Invest yourself in it!

You realize one simple thing:

The moment you do take these steps, you already manifest new levels of mutual trust in your relationship.

It takes some time and dedication to give your emotions a new "program".

Consistency is the key.

This shift won't happen overnight.

Give yourself the target to solve 90% of this issue within 1 to 3 months.

Make it your top priority at least for the first month.

Use your will power, determination and whatever you need to break through.

Invest yourself in it.

The moment you set your mind towards empowering your relationship, you invoke new refreshing forces in the core of what you share with your partner.

Take action!

You and your relationship are worth it!

# You have the power to shift your mind!

There is a common belief that your mind is somehow out of reach and that your emotions simply happen.

This is not true.

You have direct ways of accessing and shifting what happens in your mind.

Your emotions are not a given set of patterns you can't influence.

If you tend to be over jealous and you know this can destroy your love life, you are the one who will do something about it.

You are the person who has the greatest influence over your thoughts, believes, emotions, actions and attitudes.

Part of what you do is an automatic response, right?

Now, you were not born with this instinctual response.

An instinctual response is the result of a conditioning.

You simply developed a given emotional response to situations which challenge your position in a relationship.

An emotional response is not a fixed pattern.

You can change it!

Does it happen overnight?

No!

Will it take some effort, focus and dedication?

Yes!

Is it within your reach?

100% yes!!!!!

A mind pattern is a set of emotions, beliefs and thoughts.

The "jealousy" mind set is only one possible mind set in a relationship.

The "trust" mind set for instance is another one.

Even within the jealousy mind set, you can play with the way you invest yourself in it.

This is not fixed.

You can play with humor.

You can play with "playing jealous".

Most women enjoy seeing that you are ready to fight for them and for the love you share.

A bit of machismo can be welcome.

Now, if your power and jealousy weapon turns against the person you love, you obviously go one step too far.

Perfect harmony and balance in a relationship is created by a perfect combination of qualities.

You want to experiment and find out for yourself what works and what doesn't.

This book is the first step of your solution.

The real solution is to take action and apply these strategies.

Read this book again.

Go to online forums.

Share ideas with other guys.

Establish dialogue and diplomacy in your relationship.

What matters is that you don't stand still with it and keep evolving and learning.

<u>This challenge is an opportunity to grow</u>.

It is an opportunity to empower what you share with your partner.

You can come out of this closer than ever.

Accept the fact that it is a battle of forces and energies and accept as well to do what it takes to win this battle no matter what.

You are not a victim.

Your couple is not a victim.

You are simply facing one of these challenges and your goal is to win this battle.

No one needs to lose.

You can both come out of this immensely stronger and empowered!

# Part 3 – Shift unwanted jealousy in these specific cases

# How to retrain an unwanted jealousy response

Once you mentally understand the dynamics of unwanted jealousy, you still need to apply a set of behavior or attitude shifts so that the way you relate to yourself and your partner really changes.

Some of these techniques are quite challenging and upfront.

Don't be offended and stay open minded, okay?

The goal is to practice new behaviors.

The first step is to identify the triggers and situations where jealousy pops up.

If you analyze your unjustified jealousy responses, you can usually summarize them to 2 or 3 key relationship situations:

- It might be her ex calling.
- Her attitude when you go out.
- She taking off to the gym in the evening.
- Her male colleague texting her when she is with you.
- etc.

Now, identify the top 2 or 3 situations which trigger <u>unjustified jealousy</u> in you.

Write them down!

<u>Remember that we are dealing right now only with situations where your jealousy reaction is unwanted and unjustified.</u>

You now have a clear target, right?

Your goal is to shift the dynamics in these specific situations.

What we just did is very simple:

<u>We reduced the jealousy challenge to a couple of situations you can easily analyze and oversea.</u>

Instead of saying:

"I am a jealous guy and I don't know what to do..."

You are now saying something like:

"I feel uncomfortable when I see her having a chat with her ex... How can I shift my attitude so that this no longer bothers me?"

See what happened? We made it very specific!

This simplifies and reduces the challenge to a size you can easily handle!

You practice a new behavior each week for a period of 1 month until you have a whole new set of behaviors and strategies you can easily apply to replace key unwanted jealousy responses.

This gives you space to retrain max around 4 key unwanted jealousy challenges in a 30 days period (1/week).

The goal here is not to eradicate all jealousy.

As we mentioned earlier, some justified jealousy is good to maintain the strength of your relationship.

This jealousy is okay as long as you feel you are on top of that emotion rather than enslaved by it.

So, here is how this training works:

At the beginning of each week, you choose one key attitude or situation you want to work on.

It might be the fact that this male friend calls her late in the evening, the way she dresses sexy when she goes out or the fact that she is a real flirt at work for instance.

Now, imagine yourself in the specific situation you chose and practice your new "self talk" for that specific situation.

You can simulate the situation in your mind or actually consciously practice this new self talk when the situation arises.

Next time the situation arises, consciously choose to practice this new self talk.

You usually need to be confronted with a specific challenge a few times before your new self talk is truly grounded in you.

You need to use will power and force these new mind sets with determination.

Yes! This can sometimes feel like an internal battle where you reconquer your emotions with power and a winning attitude.

In the next page, I describe key situations which can trigger an unwanted jealousy response.

After each example, we identify the exact opposite empowering behaviors which might suit you best.

The goal is to create a new set of skills and attitudes you can tap into any time.

Choose the strategies that match your situation and then, apply the retraining strategy which is given to you.

You will then have a set of new skills you can apply any time you feel challenged.

The strategies or solutions I share with you are of course only suggestions.

If you take the "going partying with her girl friends" example for instance, I am not saying that you should accept it, simply that if you don't like your jealousy response, there are ways to respond in a different way.

For each situation, you are welcome to reinvent a solution which suits you best if you want to.

You are free of course!

Here are the examples I focused on in the coming chapters:

- A male friend calls her at 10 pm.
- She is a real flirt when we go out.

- She does not listen when I share my problems from work.
- She is all excited when her ex contacts her.
- She had many sex partners before me.
- She does not want to have sex when I want to.
- She goes partying with her girl friends.
- She is so open with everyone.
- He boss likes her.
- She dresses very sexy when she goes to the gym.
- I don't like the idea of her massagist touching her.

In these examples, I take the role of your inner voice and speak as if it was your inner self talk.

# A male friend calls her at 10 pm

## Unwanted jealousy response

Why is he calling now?!!! Can't he see it's 10 pm?!!!

How come she does actually pick up?

What is so urgent?

We were just in the middle of a conversation!!!

I can't stand that guy!

## Your new response

It's okay for her to have friends!

She already told me she's not romantically attracted to him.

Perfect timing to go and check the news online.

Right... I had to call Jane as well about picking up the kids on Thursday.

Time to get some fresh air!

She told me he would call.

# She is a real flirt when we go out

## Unwanted jealousy response

Why is she smiling to that guy?

How come she does not behave like that with me?

She talks with every guy except me.

What on earth does she want from them?

Isn't she happy with me?

## Your new response

Yes! But I found her first! She is mine! ☺

You stay away from my wife, bastard! ☺

I am the lucky one!

Let's be flirty too. A friend told me that this girl really likes me.

Look, I can be all smiles and charm too!

Cute waitress!!!

# She doesn't listen when I share my problems from work

## Unwanted jealousy response

She is not listening!!!

Why can't you be interested about my problems!

I bring in the cash in this house!

What are you thinking about? Your male colleague at work?

## Your new response

Fair enough! This stuff is boring anyway.

Let's focus on something romantic instead.

You're right, better clear my head and stop thinking about it.

Yes, I forgot! You already told me that you don't get the subtleties of the stock market.

# She is all excited when her ex contacts her

## Unwanted jealousy response

Are they still in contact?!!!

I am sure she still fantasies about him!

I don't want you to talk to him ever again!

He always finds an excuse to call her!

It's clear he wants her back

Why is she so f***ing friendly with him?!!!!

## Your new response

I have a past too and I like it when my ex calls me.

She already told me he was a pain to be with.

She never cheated on me and I know she never would.

He is a total loser anyway!

It's with me she is now!

Love the romantic time we had last night.

# She had many sex partners before me

## Unwanted jealousy response

Not sure if I can be with someone who had that many experiences.

I am sure she thinks I am bad at it.

Why does she have to remind of that?

Why did she have to sleep with that many guys? Is she a nympho or something?

## Your new response

532 sex partners is not that much after all!

I am dating her present, not her past.

There is not much she can do about it, can she?

It's with me she is now!

She already told me many times how much she likes what we share.

And she chose me out of 500 guys!!! I must definitely be a sex god!

# She does not want to have sex when I want to

## Unwanted jealousy response

Strange?!!! Very strange!!!!

She no longer likes me?!!

We used to be so passionate some years ago when we met.

Is she cheating or something? Maybe she has a lover she just saw today.

We never have sex anymore!!!

## Your new response

I know, she's worried about her presentation tomorrow.

I know, it's 3 am… ☺

Yes, right… We already had sex every day for the last week.

I'm off to the gym…

# She goes partying with her girl friends

## Unwanted jealousy response

This is totally unacceptable!!!!

Going out with these stupid friends who don't like me anyway.

How come I am not invited?!!!

Why does she need to go to clubs if we are together?!!!

I am sure she wants to meet someone else!

## Your new response

Great! Gives me some time to meet up with my mates!

Time to call my ex. Will be great to catch up!

I wonder how Vero is doing. Let's meet up!

Beer and game tonight! I'll have some peace at last!

I love the way she takes life! If we were spending every minute together we would end up saturated with each other.

I like my freedom too!

# She is so open with everyone

## Unwanted jealousy response

Does she really need to share that story with this stranger?

How come she talks to him as if she was ready to take off with him?

Do you have any idea of what <u>he</u> has in mind?

You are so naïve with your big smile!!!!

## Your new response

She really knows how to connect with people. A real art!

Her radiance and happiness! That's why we met in the first place!

I don't think I could ever date a boring girl!

Amazing energy!

Hey, that's Nat! Did not see her in 3 months! "Hi! How are you Nat? You look great today!"

# He boss likes her

## Unwanted jealousy response

Doesn't she see it?

Why does he call now!!!

What's going on between them?

Why is she so friendly with him?

Do you realize he is married!!!

This really pisses me off!

## Your new response

That's very good for her raise and promotion! Sure she'll get her new car now! ☺

He is really a cool guy! It must be rewarding to work with him.

Very creative team!

She already told me how much he loves his wife.

I still make more than he does.

I am the hank here.

Let's approach his wife. She is pretty cute. Let's see how he handles this...

# She dresses very sexy when she goes to the gym

## Unwanted jealousy response

We can see your legs!

Are you serious?!!!

I know exactly what guys do at the gym!

Is this what you want your fitness trainer to see?!!!

No way!!!

## Your new response

Whaou! You are a hot chick!

I can see you've been working out! I am a lucky man!

It's with me she decides to be.

You're 40 but really look like 25!

Don't touch! She's mine!

# I don't like the idea of her massagist touching her

## Unwanted jealousy response

Does she take her clothes off for the massage?

He is probably gorgeous and well built!

Why does she need a male massagist in the first place?

How come she always goes to see him in the evening when we could spend time together?

## Your new response

It is strictly professional.

It is with me that she is!

We have a great relationship and sex life.

Yes! I can trust her.

She shows me that she loves me in so many ways.

I decide to trust her!

It is childish and immature to feel jealousy in that situation.

She feels so relaxed and so hot when she comes back from her massage. I am the one who gets to enjoy her!

It is really good for her! I know she needs it to relax!

# The target? Get rid of 80% of unwanted jealousy response

This is a simple target you can focus on.

The goal is to train these new positive behaviors and reach your target within 30 days.

You know that you reach your target the moment you realize that 80% of your unwanted jealousy responses are gone.

I only described 11 key situations.

Of course, you might face a jealousy challenge which is not covered here.

If it is the case, write down a phrase or sentence summarizing your challenging situation.

Under this sentence write down "Unwanted jealousy response" and "My new response" the way I did for these previous examples.

After that, take a moment to think about what your unwanted jealousy self talk is saying.

Then, write down a few sentences which summarize what positive self talk would look like.

I know that in the beginning, it can be challenging.

Once you start, you'll notice it flows easily.

If you really don't know how or where to start, sign in for a coaching session and I'll help you further with this.

After a few weeks of practicing these self talk techniques, you can radically shift the way you respond to challenges.

Make it your top priority and focus on it actively. You'll be amazed of the results you get.

# Part 4 - Jealousy mastery

# How to use my advice

In this book, I check lots of real life situations and propose solutions for these challenges.

These are only guidelines.

These solutions are not unique.

What matters at the end is that you <u>trust and follow your instinct</u>.

Your situation is always unique.

However, certain emotional reactions and relationship patterns simply never work.

Some other patterns are usually effective.

You can become a master at playing with these behaviors and attitudes.

Remember that you are the architect of your relationship.

You are the one who decides what happens in it.

# Easy to shift jealousy? How come guys get stacked with it?

Excellent question!

Most guys tend to stay stacked with this issue because they don't see a valid enough reason to change.

For those who genuinely want to change but don't find a way to, what they miss is simply an effective strategy.

Suppose you are a jealous guy. Your first instinct is to try to suppress your jealousy response.

It's like trying to put a lid on it!

It usually does not work!

The first step is to understand more about jealousy dynamics, how they originate, why they are there in the first place, the role they play in your love life, etc.

Once you have a greater understanding of the jealousy dynamics, you respectfully reorient the power behind your jealousy and use it in a more effective way.

You learn to communicate with your girlfriend more effectively.

You discover extra sources of power in you.

You reframe your mind sets and reposition the way you stand in your relationship.

Basically, you master that power and energy!

You don't suppress it!

This is why the average guy does not usually tap into these techniques without a little guidance and support.

It is because it takes time and energy to discover all that by yourself.

I am convinced that you know already everything you will read in this book or listen to in these MP3 audios. A part of you knows it but you are not aware of it.

All these instincts we talk about are deeply buried in your subconscious mind and we simply bring them to the surface so that you can start using them.

If you prefer reinventing the wheel by yourself, you are welcome to go ahead. I do believe that if you focus on it for a few months or more, you will eventually discover some of the techniques and ideas I am about to share with you.

Even if you really dive in it by yourself without this material, you will only unveil a fraction of what you will discover in this book and MP3 audios.

The question is: do you have three months? Do you have the time and energy to do all that by yourself or do you prefer taking the direct short cut I am about to share with you.

As soon as you see the strategies I talk about, the path to master your jealousy will be crystal clear!

Again, it is not that complicate. You simply need the right set of strategies.

# I have always been the jealous type

When you say "I've always been the jealous type...", you limit yourself.

If this is the case, it is time to change your mind pattern and ideas.

Obsessive jealousy consumes and destroys relationships.

Right now, it is consuming you and wasting your energy into useless emotional loops.

A part of you defends your jealousy.

A part of you even likes it or is proud of it.

Now, you are defending the very source of your pain.

This is where the conflict lies.

For the last 10 years of your life, you lived with this pattern in your mind and probably accepted it as YOUR identity.

I 100% disagree.

Jealousy is a mind set.

It is like a shirt you put on and enjoy.

What you need to do now is find a new mind set which will give you greater satisfaction.

You need to do two things:

- The first one is to get rid of the obsessive jealousy pattern.

- The second one is to find a new mind set which works better.

If you remove your "jealousy shirt", you need to find a new identity

(You simply can't go around with a naked torso, right? ☺)

The question is:

What is the slogan you will write on your shirt?

What is the quality which is 100 times better than obsessive jealousy and which solves all your dilemmas?

The answer is "Trust".

Right now, you are constricting your girlfriend's space.

What you do when you get over jealous is keeping her on a leash.

True! I am serious.

I don't see there an expression of love.

I see an expression of control and inner fears.

This is what I see in you when you are obsessively jealous.

Does this generate harmony?

No!

Is this an expression of love?

No!

Then what is it?

It is an expression of power and control.

In fact, by being jealous you kill the very essence of what you love in her: her freedom, smile, openness, joy and life force.

All these qualities are what you are supposed to protect in her.

When you get over jealous, you do exactly the opposite: you kill them.

This is what happens.

If you love somebody, set them free (that's from "Sting...")

How do you set someone free?

By reaffirming your trust, respect and love.

When you do this, you empower your girl friend.

You give her strength, confidence.

So, what shirt will it be this morning?

The one which hurts and says "Jealousy" in screaming letters, or will it be the new pattern of "TRUST".

You do have the choice!

# How can you change if you have a bad jealousy problem?

That's the whole point, right?

Change!

The key is reconditioning!

When you get used to a certain emotional pattern like jealousy, you keep on doing it over and over again until you instruct your mind to respond in a different way.

Now, most guys give up on even trying because they don't know how or where to start!

Imagine: you spend 20 or 30 years of your life expressing a pattern which does not work!

It hurts you! It hurts your wife or girlfriend! It destroys your relationships...

All that because you did not find an exit door to that specific emotion.

I don't blame you! It is a challenge to shift a jealousy pattern when you don't know where to start.

# Can you ever change if you are the jealous type?

Of course you can!!!

Jealousy is a pattern you can influence and change!

It is simply an emotional reaction. Now, the only reason why you choose a jealous reaction is because you don't have other tools or other skills.

If I ask you: what is the alternative to a jealous response, I bet that you will have difficulties even imagining what it looks like.

It does not mean that a non jealous response does not exist! It simply means that you did not manifest it yet.

An emotional response is like a shirt you put on. If you have only one shirt, you will wear it all the time.

If you know you have a few, you will select the one you prefer, right?

If you have only one card, you keep on playing that one over and over again simply because you have no other.

So, to shift a jealousy pattern you need other options. You need to develop and train new skills!

# Isn't being jealousy a bit like being emotionally immature?

Yes! It can be, but not always.

When you grow emotionally as a man, you learn to master the jealousy patterns.

The reason guys fall into jealousy traps is simply because of lack of skills. That's all!

Sometimes, guys will believe that creating jealousy drama actually tells that you care.

In fact, it very often shows that you are trapped.

Especially if you or anyone else gets hurt in the process.

If you do express jealousy and don't feel limited by this emotion, it means that you do master it to a certain extent, which is very good.

If you and your girlfriend are happy, it usually shows that you are doing something right.

It is not jealousy itself which is immature. It is rather the way it can be used.

If you feel enslaved by an emotion you don't like, that's the sign that something is unfulfilled and that there is room for improvement.

See jealousy as a weapon or tool you can master. That's the final goal.

# I like being jealous! - Is there something wrong with me?

Not at all!

Expressing your jealousy in a wise way is an expression of your power!

What you need to check is:

How does this impact your girlfriend's life?

Are you emotionally abusive?

Are you limiting her and controlling her life?

Is she happy?

Did she threaten to leave you if you don't stop?

These are the questions you need to answer.

Jealousy is a power.

Are you abusing this power or are you using it with love and respect?

I am not here to judge any one's actions.

If you, your girlfriend and your couple are all happy, it shows that you are doing something right.

Now, if your girlfriend gets hurt by over controlling or demanding attitudes, it is usually the sign that you are going one step too far.

If it is the case, deciding to do something about it is your choice, no one else's.

# My boyfriend is super jealous! - He thinks it's just normal!

Many guys will keep on using jealousy or control until their partner tells them to stop.

Obviously this bothers them, right?

The truth is that her life belongs to her. She has the right to decide for herself what she wants.

Even when you get married, believing that this gives you the right to tell her what to do or not is a mistake.

So, why do some guys believe that it's okay for a man to limit his wife's freedom?

Well... Actually this is such an old fashioned idea now that not many people embrace such idea any more.

The power balance in couples did shift in the last 50 years depending on where you live and your cultural background.

The question now is: what to do about it?

Any time she claim your freedom back, she can face resistance.

She might go to battle and design new boundaries with you.

Now, you need to be smart with this.

Claiming her freedom is her right as a human being.

She has the right to decide for herself what she wants or doesn't want.

The moment she expresses that power and rejects her partner's authority, she is backed up by her own spirit and a force which is much vaster than herself.

Ultimately, this has to do with human dignity.

# Make sure she does not leave you over jealousy issues

Girls do break up with guys over jealousy issues.

If you don't want this to happen to you, you need to take action and get rid of whatever limits her in your relationship.

You might think: "Well, if I give her total freedom, isn't she going to cheat on me?"

What do you think?

I think it actually works the other way round!

The more you limit her, the more she'll want to run away with another guy!

Your new attitude is called trust!

You replace jealousy, possessiveness and control by a refreshing quality of trust!

Of course, you'll have a conversation in the early stages of your relationship where you define exactly what commitment means to both of you.

You could say: "I could not stand you cheating on me. I know that if it happens, we are done! I have no problem with you having male friends as long as I know you are not intimate with them. I need to be number one in your life..."

This is called setting up boundaries. You tell her what you feel is okay or not.

You talk about this a couple of times before you fully commit to each other.

She might give you a similar set of boundaries.

Once this is done, you have to set each other free!

What does this mean exactly?

You simply don't limit each other.

No control!

No demands!

Respect + Trust!

There is only one key reason why girls break up with guys: they feel limited in the relationship they are in.

When she breaks up, she says things like: "I need space!"

What she is in fact saying is: "I can't breathe! I feel limited! I am not myself anymore!"

Got it?

If you don't want this to happen to your girlfriend or wife, you want to position yourself in a way which is freeing her, not limiting her.

Are you afraid of giving her freedom? I bet you are!!!

Trusting someone is always a risk you take!

Now, trusting turns into the most exhilarating experience when you express it!

The complicity and connection which can be born from expressing that trust is absolutely thrilling.

# How to respond to jealousy triggers

When you get jealous, there is always a trigger!

The first step is to identify the trigger and the situation where jealousy pops up.

If you analyze your jealousy challenges, you will notice that you can usually summarize them to 2 or 3 key relationship situations:

- It might be her ex calling.
- Her attitude when you go out.
- She taking off to the gym in the evening.
- Her male colleague texting her when she is with you.
- etc.

Now, identify the top 2 or 3 situations which trigger jealousy in your case.

Write them down!

You now have a clear target, right?

The goal is to shift the dynamics in that specific situation.

You can either:

- Educate her and get her to shift her behavior.

or

- Shift the way you respond to that specific trigger.

This last option will usually be the way to go for a guy.

Why? Because that's what usually gives you the best long lasting results.

What we just did is very simple:

We reduced the jealousy challenge to a couple of situations you can easily analyze and oversea.

Instead of saying: "I am a jealous guy and I don't know what to do..."

You are now saying: "I feel uncomfortable when I see her having a chat with her ex... How can I shift my attitude so that this no longer bothers me?"

See what happened? We made it very specific!

This simplifies and reduces the challenge to a size you can easily handle!

# Why getting rid of unwanted jealousy is so thrilling!

Have you ever been in a dream where you feel trapped?

Do you remember the exciting relief when you wake up?

You realize that there is a way out!

This is how it feels to solve the jealousy riddle!

Of course, you don't want to look at it when you believe that there is no way out or that you have to go through 5 years of therapy to solve it.

Now, imagine what happens when you realize that jealousy challenges can be rapidly solved without you loosing your power!

Do you feel this clear freshness waking up in your mind. You suddenly perceive a whole new set of possibilities for you and your girlfriend.

Open doors!

That's how it feels!

Part of you might not believe that this is possible?

Well! It is!

I am not fooling you around!

This is your life and the challenge you face is a big deal! Really! I am aware of it!

This is important!

It takes some courage to trust and believe in yourself!

I don't know you but I believe in you!

I believe in your power and infinite potential!

I know that because you set up your mind to it you are easily winning this battle.

And guess what?

Once you achieve this specific victory, you can focus on new aspects of your life which really matter.

There is a whole world of possibilities for your refreshed couple.

Grab this opportunity now and don't let go! This is your chance!

# How men give away their power and try getting it back

The more power you give away to your girlfriend or wife, the more you try to get it back through jealousy, insecurity or controlling patterns.

See your individual base as an entity.

You feel secure when you are in control of that base.

The moment you get into a relationship you often give too much of that power to your new partner.

You simply give her the right to have control over your actions, thoughts, time frame, attitudes, etc.

This power transfer is mainly unconscious.

You believe it is right to make concessions and go with what she wants rather than what you want.

This is how many men lose their power!

They simply give it up!

You end up giving her the control seat in your life.

Now, what are the consequences of that?

On your side, it tends to generate insecurity and greater desire to control her.

This gets expressed in jealousy patterns as well.

The reason why you want to control her life is because you simply want to gain back what you gave her.

Imagine that you have a certain reserve of controlling power.

When you are single, you express this in your own life.

You use this controlling power to protect your freedom and stay in charge of what is yours.

Now, when you get into a relationship and you allow her to step in and control some aspects of your own personal life (like career choices, activities, food choices, clothes, social life, etc) you end up with an extra unused reserve of controlling power.

The most natural way to express this controlling power is often to project it into her own life and start trying to control some aspects of her existence, get over jealous or very insecure.

This is when your couple gets in trouble.

Realize that you express insecurity towards her simply because you feel you are no longer in charge of your own life.

Therefore you start relying on her to provide you with this security.

If she decides to go on a date with her ex, you end up with a big power gap and feelings of anxiousness and insecurity because you gave your power away earlier and don't have the resources now to emotionally protect yourself.

When she goes on a date with her ex or flirts with other man, you end up with no control over either you or her.

Can you see these power dynamics?

They are very organic and instinctual.

It is almost like an equation which needs to be balanced.

So, what is the solution to all that?

It is actually quite simple!

If you don't want insecurity, controlling patterns or jealousy to rise in your being, stay in charge of your life!

Don't give her the control seat!

Don't delegate your power and don't let her choose what is right for you!

You need to stay in charge of your own life!

This is a decision you take in the very early stages of your relationship.

Don't give up your power!

The next question is:

How do you build up a relationship without giving up your power? Is it even possible?

Of course it is!

# Justified jealousy and when it's okay to express it

In some situations, expressing your jealousy is very good.

Suppose that you are out with her and she starts talking about her ex.

In fact, it happened many times before.

It became a pattern.

She praises what he does or what they did in the past.

It feels draining for you!

Should you say something?

Of course you should!

"I don't really want to hear about your ex. Is this okay with you? Thank you"

This is called a boundary.

It protects the time you have together.

When you educate her or express a boundary, you need to be firm and consistent.

You might need as well to repeat the same message a few times until she truly gets it.

You can take as well a special moment later to tell her exactly why you no longer want to hear about her ex.

Her talking about an ex again and again is one example.

Here are some more situations which can trigger a positive jealousy response:

- She keeps a portrait of her and her ex which everyone can see in the house where you live together.

- She talks a lot about a specific male friend.
- She picks up a call and spends 30 min on the phone when you are out having dinner together.
- She frequently cancels dates with you at the last minute because of work.
- Etc.

As you can see, not all these situations would be called "jealousy" issues.

What they have in common though is that, your girlfriend's attitude is tactless and you can educate her.

Some even more obvious positive jealousy responses happen when she cheats or lies to you.

You can as well express positive jealousy towards a guy who definitely comes too close to her and does not respect your couple.

The first question to ask yourself is:

"Is this a situation in which jealousy is justified or not?"

Now, in 95% of the cases, jealousy is unjustified.

It means that guys tend to overreact, mistrust and blow up a potentially nice evening without good reason.

This is why most of the male jealousy strategies are focused on shifting your response rather than educating her.

Use positive jealousy and educate her only in some isolated and exceptional situations.

This attitude must represent less than 5% of what you share with her.

Why? Because that's the maximum she can usually take!

Every now and then (max once a month!) you have an opportunity and a need to ask her to shift something in the way she relates to you.

Remember that educating her happens only in some exceptional cases!

In most situations, shifting your own response and respecting her freedom is what works best!

<u>If you overused jealousy and control in the past, forget even totally about trying to educate her on anything for a while, at least until you deal with your own issues!</u>

# MIRROR TACTICS! - Do EXACTLY what she does!

I call these "Mirror tactics".

Suppose that in your opinion, she's too flirty with a guy at a social event.

Instead of going after her, find a girl and do the same. Flirt!

Make it obvious and don't hold back.

This will most probably trigger a reaction on her side.

You see, most women will defend their right to be open and free with anyone until you start being open and free too.

That's when it hits them.

They feel it too: the insecurity!

They feel the jealousy emotions kicking in.

Mirroring her behavior is one of the best ways to let her see how it feels to be in your shoes.

You don't pressure her. You don't express your jealousy to her.

Instead, you do EXACTLY what she does.

If this triggers a conversation and she's angry at you for flirting with another girl, here is what you say next:

"So, you don't like it when I flirt with another girl?"

"Why not?"

"How does that make you feel?"

"I thought you too were having a good time with that idiot tonight"

"Would you say that we were both engaging in flirting or connecting with someone else?"

"So, if I stop flirting with other girls, does that mean you have to stop flirting with other guys too?"

Now, that's usually when it hits her!

This simple realization will often trigger the behavior changes you want in her.

She will do it because she knows that she doesn't like it when the situation is reversed.

She respects you.

She doesn't want to hurt you.

Now, she knows BY EXPERIENCE how her flirting with another guy makes YOU feel.

Next time you go out, you might feel her staying CONSCIOUSLY closer to you out of her OWN choice.

There was no demand! There was no pressure.

Guys come to me ALL THE TIME with this type of breakthrough when they use these mirror tactics.

They work amazingly well to get her to shift a behavior in her own terms.

In most cases, what's interesting is that if you had tried to "force" that behavior change on her, it would probably have triggered fights or tension.

Now, because it is her decision and she came to that conclusion by herself, that's a totally different story.

She embraces that choice rather than resenting it!

The other essential point for you to understand is that when she shifts a behavior, YOU trigger that positive change in her by NOT challenging her on this issue and GIVING her space to change it IF she wants to on her own time and terms.

Very impressive when this happens.

Please email me your success story when you get such break through, ok?

Would love to hear it!

http://vitalcoaching.com/contact.htm

# Call me instead of unloading your insecurities on her

Once you start working with these jealousy files you will see that most of the strategies to handle the situations you face are already written and in a way, you are already using them.

All you might need now is someone who helps you stay focused when delusional or unjustified fears kick in.

The worst you can do is to go to her for help when this happens.

Remember that she's not your therapist.

It's not her job to reassure you systematically, especially if these episodes are frequent.

So, here is the strategy I want to share with you:

Call me!

My number is on my site:

http://vitalcoaching.com/contact.htm

Here is what I suggest you do:

Next time, you have an episode where you feel insecure or jealous, pick up the phone and call me for an unscheduled power kick!

If you get my voice mail, you leave me a message and I'll call you back as soon as I can.

It is that simple.

It will give you a safe space to share what's happening and we'll check together the best strategy to handle this.

What I give you is more power.

This is not therapy, ok! I think you are perfectly fine! This is about performance and life mastery and this is EXACTLY what I can help you with.

I have a few clients I coach that way on jealousy issues and we end up having non scheduled sessions every now and then.

I might speak with them maybe a couple times a month.

Sometimes, I don't hear from them for a few weeks or months.

This is it. You won't get broke and I can tell you that the results I see happening in these guys are amazing.

The advantage of having me on call that way is that you don't bring these issues to your girlfriend. In a way you keep her out of it which REALLY protects your couple.

In my opinion, this is by far the best way to go...

Yes, you'll need to get some coaching credits - My services are not free and I know it is an investment.

However it is well worth it and I made it very easy and totally affordable for you.

Check it out on my site:

http://vitalcoaching.com/coaching.htm

# How to stay cool always! No matter what she does!

Staying cool is an attitude you train!

You prepare yourself for the absolute worst and imagine how you would react if you were the coolest person on this planet.

What would you do?

What would you say?

Expressing insecurities in relationships is a lack of emotional maturity.

It simply says that your mind and personal power are not strong enough yet!

Yes! The goal is to always be in a positive and uplifting state of mind no matter what.

If you go out together and already know the triggers that could lead to a fight or tension between the two of you, you prepare yourself before they even happen.

You DECIDE not to respond before the situation even arises.

I agree with you, it takes focus and determination to achieve just that.

But guess what? This is part of your life mastery training. This is how you become a better person and grow character.

This is how you become a partner she enjoys and wants to spend her time with.

To your power!

# Part 5 - Right boundaries

# Build up peace! Give her space to relax!

When your irritation threshold is very low, your girlfriend walks on egg shells all the time!

She can't relax!

She must be ready for an attack and on the defensive all the time!

This is exhausting after a while!

You simply need to increase your tolerance level and give her space to relax.

Creating peace and harmony in your relationship is something you do consciously by choice!

# Defend her freedom

If you want to remember one thing from this material, this is it!

<u>Defend her freedom!</u>

Defend her happiness!

Defend her rights!

If you are looking for a new way of expressing your power, this is the exact shift you need to make.

It is not overprotecting!

It is not being afraid for her!

It is stimulating and defending what you care for the most in her:

Her joy and pleasure to be alive!

If you crush that, you crush part of yourself!

When you express jealousy, you use what you can call "controlling power".

When you defend her freedom, you use your "protective power".

What is the difference?

Controlling power limits!

Protective power opens doors!

This is the exact way to express your power in the future.

You are not dropping your power, you are expressing it differently!

There are two key ways you can approach nature: as a hunter or as a defender!

The same applies to women!

You have two ways you can love her:

- By closing your arms around her and limiting her.

Or

- Opening your arms around her and giving her space and freedom.

These two approaches are totally different.

So many men and couples are trapped in the first model!

It is much more challenging to love unconditionally and sponsor her freedom and destiny no matter what.

If you are looking for another channel to use your infinite source of power, this is it!

Protect, sponsor and defend her freedom!

This is the true alternative to jealousy patterns.

Ask yourself:

- Do you want her to be with you because you force her to?

Or

- Do you want her to be with you because she is free and chooses to?

By the way, you can replace the word "freedom" by "happiness", "destiny line", "joy", "pleasure to be alive" or anything you feel inspired to.

Defend her freedom!

# How she will react to pressure and demands

If you say something like:

"I don't want you to be so open with everyone when we go to social events! I don't like it! It makes me VERY uncomfortable!"

What's the usual emotional response to that?

Will she be cool and say something like:

"Sure, I didn't realize I was crossing the line - I'll be happy to change my behavior - What you want is very important to me."

Or will she say something like:

"Are you telling me what to do now? Whaou! I can't believe this! You actually used to like it when I was fun and outgoing! Now you want me to become the wall paper girl who says nothing? Why on earth do you ask me to do something like that?"

You guessed right!

In most cases, SHE WILL REBEL!

She will fight back, attack you and defend her right to do whatever she wants.

Why is that?

Why is it that she doesn't see your point?

Here is the answer:

It is because in a subtle way, you are not just asking her to change something in her, you are as well:

- Accusing her
- Limiting her freedom
- Demanding
- Projecting an emotionally loaded request
- Telling her that she's not good enough

- Saying that she's doing something wrong
- Etc.

How do YOU react when someone attacks you?

Do you just give in or do you fight back?

Do you engage in a constructive feed back conversation or do you cave in and retreat?

See the point?

There is a way of communicating with her which works 100 times better than demands!

Here we go:

"I face a challenge and I don't know what to do about it... Want to help me with that? What do you suggest?"

What happened there?

You asked for her opinion and input.

You design a solution TOGETHER!

That's a totally different story, right?

Here is the line you can use next time you have a feed back chat with her:

"What do you suggest?"

# Don't use your controlling power to limit her

If you are a guy who carries lots of power with him.

If professionally and materially, you have a VERY good base and you are in charge of your existence.

Being in that place does involve control over what is yours.

Now, when you are in a relationship, there is a natural risk to use the same type of controlling force on her.

These mental and emotional jealousy patterns, whether you express them verbally or not are an expression of your controlling power.

The thing is that this controlling power can precisely kill what you love the most.

You know that already of course.

You don't want to alienate your girlfriend, isolate her or make her feel miserable.

Of course you won't go that way.

Imagine just for a second that you would express all the jealousy patterns and controlling impulses that raise in your mind, it would be a nightmare for her, right?

What does this tell you?

That this controlling power is dangerous for your relationship.

It is literally a fire that can burn down your couple.

You know that already. I am saying this to reinforce a fact you are already familiar with.

The key idea is to use your power wisely!

It usually means PROTECTING MORE while CONTROLLING LESS.

You can protect what you care for without losing a sense of ownership over what happens in your relationship.

In another article we'll check very specific ways to use your protective power instead of your controlling one.

# Use your protective force rather than control

You see positive expressions of protective power all the time in society!

It shows up when:

- A boss gives you space to be creative at your job.
- A mother watches her child playing in the park.
- You let a dog run freely while keeping an eye on what it does.
- We redirect the flow of a river so that a village doesn't get hit with the next storm.
- Etc.

In all these expressions, people are STILL using their power!

It is not control.

It is protection!

- You don't limit the employee's creativity.
- You don't hold the child by the hand.
- You don't keep the dog on the leash.
- You don't stop the river from flowing.

What's the result?

LIFE FLOWS!

It's not being stopped or limited!

That's one of the most subtle distinctions you can make when using your power in life.

How much control is REALLY needed to keep you safe.

Do you need 5 locks or just one?

Do you really need a high fence?

See the point?

In your relationship, controlling power is a joy killer!

It destroys spontaneity and complicity because what partners really tell each other when they use it is:

"I don't trust you! I don't think you are grown up enough to make your own decisions!"

Using control on your partner usually means SERIOUS TROUBLE!

What's the alternative if you don't want to lose your power?

Well, you still can use your power but in a different way.

When dealing with relationship boundaries, you will say things like:

- "Looks like this guy was really into you" rather than "I don't want you to speak with him again!"
- If you see her chatting with another man, you approach them and say:
- "Who is your friend" rather than "Do you always need to flirt with guys like that when we are out???"

If she looks super sexy when taking off to the gym, you'll say:

- "Whaou! You look like a bombshell - I am so glad I am the one you have sex with" rather than "You are not planning to go to the gym dressed like that, are you?!"

These subtle distinctions are essential if you want to really connect with your partner.

Protective power? She'll enjoy it!

Controlling or limiting power? She'll rebel!

What's your choice?

# Her sexiness is precisely what attracts you in her

A woman's happiness is VERY precious.

When I interview guys on this topic, they often say that what got them attracted to their girlfriend are her smile and radiance.

It is the fact that she looked happy, fun and outgoing.

That's a trait you DON'T want your girlfriend to lose! Believe me!

That's what brings joy to your relationship and makes it fun to be with her.

The moment you kill that, you destroy what you care for the most.

You need to manage your jealousy without destroying these qualities in her.

As a life partner, your job is to protect her freedom and happiness, not to destroy them!

So, how do you manage that specific tricky challenge?

You trust her and tell her what the TRUE boundary is.

The true boundary is: "Don't get intimate with another man - If you do, I'm out"

That's usually the deal breaker in relationships.

95% of couples agree with this subtle and often unspoken agreement.

The other 5% of couples will have an open relationship or some higher degree of sexual freedom.

Listen, when she's happy and even flirty, what bothers you is not so much what happens there, it is the potential of what COULD follow up.

Guys get jealous because they IMAGINE what COULD happen next.

Of course if you see her flirting with another guy, it might bother you a bit.

But what really gets to you is if they establish a connection that can lead to something else.

She needs to know what your EXACT boundary is:

"No intimacy with another man"

Once she knows, give her space and trust her!

# Being clingy or desperate is a big turn off for women

Women can love freedom and independence.

In fact when a man has a high level of inner power and autonomy it gives her trust and the assurance that he will be able to protect her in challenging situations.

Women often rely on men for emotional security.

A man who is strong and confident is magnetically attractive.

When you are extremely possessive and jealous of her every move, you sound very desperate.

It is a huge turn off for her.

Having to constantly feed a man's emotional needs can be very demanding for a woman.

It creates pressure and limits her within the relationship.

The alternative is to stay in power.

Stay in charge of your own life.

In most cases, the best way to create long term harmony in the relationship is to maintain a strong personal base.

When you "abandon" yourself in a relationship, you become very vulnerable.

Stay in control of your life.

Go beyond the "exclusively passionate dream".

Stay awake!

Keep your survival and fighting skills alive.

If you transfer all your power to your partner and simply rely on her for validation and security, this kills your self worth and personal power.

Don't give up your personal independence and own destiny line.

No need to sacrifice yourself.

When you challenge yourself, you empower your own vehicle.

You don't wait for your partner to show up.

You go on and follow up with your life.

Action is life force.

Action is what gives you extra confidence and deletes unwanted jealousy.

Join forces with your partner, sure, <u>but don't give up your individual identity</u>.

Make sure that you are able to stand on your own any time.

This immensely empowers the relationship on the long term.

# Are you committed or not?

If you are a jealous guy, this is probably the first question to ask yourself.

Why?

Because the only reason that does justify jealousy is if you need to protect the territory of your relationship.

This is how the jealousy instinct was created in the first place.

If you are non committed, being jealous is a waste of time and energy.

You try to protect something that does not exist.

On top of that, you do violate her most basic human right: her right for freedom!!!

Conclusion?

In that situation, being jealous is a waste of your precious time!

# Is excessive jealousy emotional abuse?

Definitely yes!!!

A woman is emotionally abused when a man tries to control her life, steals her freedom, limits her, and tells her what to think, wear or feel!!!

These are definitely abusive situations.

How bad are these patterns? It simply depends on the intensity!

If you are a guy and you discover abusive patterns like these, you need to educate yourself and shift these behaviors.

# Is a little jealousy good in a relationship?

Of course it is!

The question is not whether you can express jealousy.

The real question is: are you in control of your jealousy or does your jealousy control you?

Jealousy is simply a tool!!! It is a weapon.

If you know how to use it effectively it will positively impact on your relationship.

Now, if you see that your controlling attitudes are destroying your partner's joy, it's obviously the sign that you already went a few steps too far.

Women love it when they see their partners really caring for them.

Being a bit jealous here and there is a good way of showing that you care.

But!!!! It's essential that you stay on top of that emotion and play your jealousy card as a game.

You use it when you want and can withdraw it whenever you want.

This is the real skill you need to develop.

Don't be the slave of your jealousy! Be its master!

# Why does she try to make you jealous?

Most of the times, it is a teasing game.

Nothing serious.

It is a way of flirting.

It is a seduction game.

It is a good sign.

It is a sign that there is complicity and that she wants to seduce you.

If you are offended by it, it blows up the game.

Instead, play the game:

Make her jealous as well.

If she is really trying to hurt you, it is of course another story.

Can you see that?

Making you jealous is her way of wanting your attention.

If you do this yourself to a woman, it is a seduction game.

It is part of the flirting game.

You make her come closer and then playfully reject her.

You do this to wake up her desire and even to stimulate sexual tension between the two of you.

It is a game.

Enjoy it!

# If she talks a lot about other men

Educate your partner!

Talking about other men when she is in a relationship or on a date with you is a lack of dating skills.

It is a lack of tact.

You don't need to hear that. The fantasies which go on in her mind are okay as long as she doesn't picture them for you.

Tell her! Design a new boundary in your relationship.

Tell her until she gets it and shifts her attitude.

Going on a date with you is about you, the two of you, not her and someone else.

It is your right to establish a new boundary.

Tell her: "I would rather talk about something else. Is it okay with you?"

If you enjoy her love stories, it is different of course.

However, if this wakes up unwanted jealousy in you, tell her you don't want to hear that.

Simple and direct!

When you are on a date, it is nice to feel valued.

It is about what you two have in common.

Educate her on that.

It is okay.

Repeat the message until she gets it.

# She must respect your personal space

When you live together, you are the owners of the space you live in.

You do this together.

Having pictures of her ex around the house is not the best way to validate your relationship.

Your house is dedicated to one thing: <u>your partnership</u>

This means that your task is to preserve and protect your personal space.

If she wants to keep memories or old letters from past relationships, you can't stop her. However, you can make sure that she keeps all that with her personal things.

You have the right to have some control over what happens in your personal space.

So, dare to express that power.

This is definitely okay as long as you are not trying to control her actions, beliefs or emotions.

If you have your own house and live separately, the same applies: ultimately you are the one who decides what happens in your home and what comes in or not.

Obsessive jealousy comes from a need to secure your life.

You know she is a window into your existence and you don't want to lose control.

This is why you tend to limit her freedom.

Now, the moment you gain back full control over your personal space, you gain back a very high level of security.

<u>This is your right</u>.

It is healthy to stay in charge of your personal environment.

If you live together, you share this authority.

You express this authority by taking decisions together, talking about boundaries and limits and using diplomacy when you discover an area of tension or conflict.

# Have a constructive chat on relationship boundaries with her

One of the best ways to strengthen you couple is to find out EXACTLY what is ok and what is not in your relationship.

You will often uncover that you both pretty much want the same.

Here are some ideas to start a conversation on boundaries:

- "How physical do you think it is ok for us to be with other people?"
- "Would it bother you if I was flirty with another girl in your presence?"
- "What exactly would bother you?"
- "Do you feel that the same boundary must apply to both of us or just one of us?"
- Etc.

This is a constructive conversation because there is no finger pointing or accusation.

You are not telling her what to do

You ask for feed back.

You ask open ended questions.

You ask her to share.

This is why it gives her space to express what she feels.

The result? You design boundaries TOGETHER!

Because she designed the solution together with you, she embraces that choice rather than resenting it!

# How often can you have a serious talk with her?

If you already had a constructive discussion just a couple days ago, wait al least one to two weeks before you have another boundaries discussion.

Your couple can digest some "processing" but if you do it too frequently you don't give each other enough time and space to integrate new behaviors.

So, if you already had a serious chat recently, don't bring it up again even if something new comes up.

Instead, make a note of it and keep track of the points you would like to discuss when you have your next boundary chat.

You can journal on these issues.

Write down what works for you and what doesn't.

When a new element appears, keep track of it don't bring it up straight away in a reactive way.

It is way better to wait for a few days until you can sit down again with her for a new in depth "boundary conversation".

# She's doing it again! - Why doesn't she listen?

If you agreed on something and she crosses the line again, relax and give her some space and time to integrate this new behavior.

Sometimes it takes some repetition and revisiting the same issue a few times before new behaviors are really implemented.

Don't be too impatient with her. She's a human being!

Give her space for imperfections.

It's ok.

Next time she does something you disapprove of, repeat this mantra to yourself:

"She is not perfect and that's ok".

"I am not perfect either".

# How do you deal with jealousy in a long distance relationship?

Long distance means that you have all the challenges of a normal relationship + the distance.

The fact that you can't check what your girlfriend or wife is doing means that you need to multiply your level of trust.

The way to solve unwanted jealousy is the same as if you were living together. You simply need to empower your "trust muscle" and reinforce extra qualities like respect and freedom.

With the internet communication tools like webcam chat and email, distance is no longer what it used to be.

Every now and then, have a deep conversation to see if your relationship is actually giving you both what you want.

If you notice a sign of dissatisfaction, you need to take action and make sure that your relationship stays exciting even with the distance.

How to make and keep your relationship exciting is a whole different topic.

The first step though is how to tame a jealousy response when it appears and turn it into trust.

# Why supporting her financially makes you prone to jealousy

Yes! Taking financial responsibility for her can make you more prone to jealousy outbursts.

It opens a door!

It increases your expectations!

It makes you feel that you have the right to tell her what to do or not.

In other terms, it radically shifts the dynamics of how you relate to her.

What is the solution?

Does it mean that if you don't want to feel jealousy, you must not give her money?

Does it mean that if she wants to start her own business and you have the resources, you must not help her?

Well...

Ask yourself this question:

What is the deal?

What do you expect in return?

Would you still give her this money if she wants to go partying with her male friends or go on dates with her ex?

Really! What is the deal?

Is it a gift or a loan?

What if you break up or she meets someone else?

Will you still give her money?

How will this affect you emotionally?

Usually, having this financial link makes challenges harder to deal with.

If you are both financially and materially independent, you manifest a higher level of freedom.

What is left between the two of you is really love and attraction!

These are the true binding forces!

Now, if the core binding force is a financial agreement you end up playing a very different game.

What will she say if you don't want to help her financially?

"No money? No girlfriend!"

Would this be her answer?

Or would it sound more like:

"Money is not an issue between the two of us. I thank you for your honesty and I'll find another way of supporting myself. It changes nothing between you and me. I love you for who you are, not for whatever money or support you would have given me!"

How would your girlfriend respond?

Dare to ask yourself this question and face the facts, whatever these facts are.

So, what does this have to do with jealousy?

You can see the money you give her as an investment.

You invest your money into a part of your being or an aspect of your life you care for.

You usually expect something in return, whether it's conscious or unconscious.

You realize that if you give her money, it is not just a free gift.

There are usually unspoken conditions and you do expect some form of commitment on her side.

Because you give more (not just love), you expect more!

Now, she might not realize or even accept this.

Is she saying?

"Because you support me financially, it gives you the right to tell me what to do"

Of course not!

The unspoken contract is never discussed in detail! It stays very vague!

This is why supporting her financially can mean trouble for your relationship.

Because this agreement is unspoken and there is no clear "contract" you are left only with powers like jealousy and control to enforce it.

This is why giving her money can make you more prone to jealousy.

It is simply a natural instinctual response to this situation.

Like with any other jealousy triggers, increased awareness is already a big part of the solution.

You can avoid the trigger altogether or face it with greater awareness and new tools.

You have two choices:

- The first one is to pull back and make sure that you are both materially and financially independent.

Or

- You can of course support her financially if you want to, and make sure that you are very clear about what you expect in return.

Both directions can work.

If you are faced with this situation, trust your instincts and keep these ideas in mind when making your final choice.

If you still did not take the step, you can as well offer her some financial support and observe if this messes up the connection that you have.

If it does you can always pull back and decide not to it again in the future.

# How datable is she?

Some girls simply don't want to be committed!

They like their freedom and won't make concessions on that, which is fine!

If you show up in their lives and try to make them be exclusive, you crash!

Your two plans don't match!

She has her agenda!

You have yours!

They don't match!

When you start dating a girl, you can easily identify if she is someone who will commit or not.

You will see warning signs:

- She does not return your calls!
- She lies!
- Talks a lot about exes and sexual adventures.
- She gets loads of male attention when you take her out and forgets about you.
- She is young and openly says she wants to explore her sexuality.
- She dresses very sexy and is obviously on a hunt!
- Etc.

When guys see these signs, they usually reject or deny them.

They think:

"She is confusing!"

"She gives me mixed signals!"

"I don't fully get her!"

When in fact, she is crystal clear!

She is saying exactly what she wants and confirms this with her actions and attitudes.

The fact that she goes out with you a couple of times does not mean that she wants to commit!

You might assume this but it is not her intention at all!

Maybe she even wants to fool herself and believe it is exclusively with you she wants to be while dating other guys at the same time!

She might say things like:

"We are so good together!"

"I love you!"

"I am so glad we met!

She might even get jealous and make a scene over you calling your ex!

This is the moment you need to be really smart as a guy!

Very often these few signs I just described don't mean commitment!

They mean: there is something nice going on!

Your next step is to look at her actions! They speak louder than words!

Does this mean you can't date her? Of course you can!

You can date her but in a light and non committed way.

We are now talking about a very specific type of girl who enjoys her freedom and likes it that way.

She is not asking for change!

My guess is that probably 1/5 of the girls you can meet fit in that category.

This is what you need to recognize in the early stages.

Why?

Because her behaviors can quickly trigger a flow of unwanted jealousy in you.

You feel jealous because you believe she is committed when in fact she is not!

This can confuse you and drive you into an emotional roller coaster.

That's the last thing you want.

Remember that if she is not committed to you, your jealousy is unjustified.

You can play with that emotion of course but there is no "territory" to defend.

Expressing jealousy and possessiveness will most likely mess up your connection and drive her away.

If she likes her freedom, she has probably been confronted before with guys who tried to control her. She often has strategies ready to get rid of them, believe me!

The only way to stick around is to respect her choices. If you don't, you are asking for trouble, guaranteed!

# Part 6 - Her exes, male friends and world

# Tell her that I don't like her being in touch with ex?

The first thing to check is: when did you have your last "boundaries" discussion with her?

If it's more than a month, it is possible to sit down again and have an open heart discussion about this.

If you want a chat, instead of saying: "When you interact with him, I don't like it and I think you should stop..."

Say:

"Let's chat about exes today... How close do you feel it is appropriate for them to be? For instance would you be ok with me exchanging text messages with my ex in the evening while you and I are together?"

"What do you feel is ok or not - What's your opinion? I am really interested in knowing what you think..."

Remember that you don't tell her what to do.

You simply bring it up in an open way and let her see what could be a win for both of you.

When you have this chat, keep it short and targeted.

Let her see that you are ok with whatever direction she wants to take.

However, she must know that if she connects with her ex it means that you might stay in touch with your exes as well in similar ways. Would she be ok with that?

Another opportunity to practice your favorite mirror tactics ;)

# She keeps pictures of her exes

Her past relationships are part of her life. It is her past.

Having some memories of this past is okay as long as this does not keep you from evolving together.

If you don't want to see these pictures, ask her to keep them with her own stuff. Fair enough!

I mean, would she be pleased if you were hanging a picture of your ex on the living room's wall?

It is healthy for her to do what she wants with her personal stuff.

This is a place where she has the right to express her control.

Let it go and don't be bothered. That's of course unless all this is in your face. Then it is okay to tell her.

Put it this way: even though she keeps some pictures of her exes, it is with you she is today.

# Is it okay for her to have a male friend?

The answer is yes!

The number one reason for break ups is too much control within the relationship.

If your relationship becomes too constricting or limiting, sooner or later you either explode or become very unhappy and drained.

A relationship is a place where you encourage mutual freedom.

The real base of your relationship is not mutual control; it is mutual trust and love.

When you commit yourself to your partner, you usually decide to be sexually exclusive.

This is the real boundary.

Now, boundaries are designed consciously.

You talk about them and find out a good balance which works for both of you.

For instance, some couples consciously decide to have an open relationship because they feel they need a greater level of freedom within what they share.

What is important is to design these boundaries together.

Dialogue! Diplomacy!

These are the best ways to design healthy relationship boundaries.

When you are obsessively jealous, your relationship boundaries become immensely constricting.

I encourage you to relax about her male friends and realize this simple fact:

It is still with you she decides to be.

It is with you she shares her life.

It is with you she is intimate.

So, it's simple!

Drop it and trust her!

This is a gift of freedom you give to each other.

Dare to empower her with your trust.

Trying to control her social life is a no-win situation.

It is a dead end which leads to increased fights and break up.

Increase the level of freedom within your relationship to make sure that your partnership breathes and does not get asphyxiated.

Allow other men to validate her.

What this tells to your relationship is that she is a great woman.

It tells that she has the choice but it is with you she decides to be.

This is the best way to perceive her interactions with other men.

# How to deal with her having male friends

Is it okay for your partner to have male friends? Sure it is.

It validates her and refreshes your relationship.

You have two options:

- Be controlling demanding and freaking out.

Or

- Letting it go and even enjoying it

The real alternative is for you to have female friends as well.

Again, open communication is what works best.

Talk about it with your partner and find out about your real boundaries.

The rules are the same for both.

If she can't take it, then obviously there is no reason for you to take it either.

Limiting each other's space kills the relationship.

Staying in touch with good friends and having time off out of the relationship is healthy.

It is of course a slight challenge and a stretch of your comfort zone but it is worth it.

On the long term everyone benefits from it.

Remember, it is still with you she decides to be.

You stay number one.

# What to do when you see her chat with someone else

Imagine you are at a party and you see her having a chat with a man.

Simple, stop watching and take action.

If she is focused on someone else, the best response is for you to focus on someone else as well.

Don't wait for her to come back.

Go and engage a conversation with another woman as well.

Your partner can only give you so much validation.

What gives you extra power is validation from other women as well.

Connect, exchange and open up.

The best way to overcome obsessive jealousy is to gain extra power and satisfaction.

If you are the "closed" type, challenge yourself and connect; even if you feel slight discomfort with it.

Don't limit yourself. Don't isolate yourself.

Stay active socially and yes, it's okay to speak with another woman.

Don't feel guilty about it.

You are not betraying anyone by sharing a couple of words with another girl.

You are expressing a basic human need: exchange and communication.

When you get validation from other women, this boosts your self esteem and empowers you.

One of the reasons you can get clingy or dependent from your partner's attention is because you believe that no other female can value you as a man.

<u>Give other women the opportunity to share a moment with you.</u>

The moment you get a smile from another woman, it gives you an essential confidence boost.

Don't isolate yourself. Don't limit yourself.

Open up and connect.

A light chat with a nice woman is perfectly okay.

You are not betraying your partner when going for it.

# Discuss your insecurities if she chats with other guys?

Well, the question is: Do you even want to discuss it?

Did she cheat?

Did she betray you?

Did she do something wrong?

Or do you simply feel insecure?

I mean, is this issue in her hands or in your hands?

Is she your therapist or your lover?

Girls tend to get tired of having to reassure their partner endlessly.

It's exhausting to feel that no matter how hard you try, your partner still believes you are going to cheat on him.

So, the solution is to get things straight once and for all:

What are your relationship boundaries?

Are you committed to each other?

This type of questions.

Once these are solved, don't keep on bringing them over and over again each time she has a chat with a guy.

If you still have problems with it, it means that you need to work on this issue on your side and do what it takes to turn a jealousy response into trust.

# She's got male friends but I have no female friends

This is to follow up on the previous article about her after work drinks with male colleagues...

The key is not so much about developing deep friendships, it is about interacting with the opposite sex.

So, you don't have to build a strong friendship with a female friend.

Even though you are in a relationship, keep interacting with other women:

- Flirt a bit.
- Chat with a girl you just met.
- Activate your social power when attending an event.
- Etc.

Once you realize that other women like you too, your level of power and confidence is REALLY boosted.

When you rely only on your girlfriend or wife for female validation, this makes you very dependent on her.

The moment she transfers a bit of her attention to another guy, even if it is for a couple of hours and there is for sure nothing going on, you still feel insecure and left out because she is all you have.

Now, if the moment she comes back home, she sees you on Facebook chatting with an old female friend who just found you back, the balance is shifted instantly!

Let's get this right, ok?

The goal here is not to make her jealous. The goal is to have other sources of social validation in your life, not just your partner.

That's the key!

# Jealous of the men she works with

Is your partner a flirt?

Is she surrounded by a couple of attractive colleagues?

The question is: What can you do about it?

Maybe you too take some lessons with an attractive fitness trainer.

Maybe you have a secret crush on one of your colleagues.

These situations happen in life.

Can you stop them from happening? No. It is simple.

You need to keep on living.

Light flirts are okay as long as you don't act on them.

It is okay for your partner to have contact with other men, even if they are handsome and very attractive.

The truth is that she is with you.

It is with you she decides to be.

Spending time with others is healthy. It is part of life to work with others.

This won't change.

What you can change is the way you stand in it.

Communicate openly with your partner. There is no taboo!

The moment you can share and tease each other with it, you bring this whole issue to something very light and even fun.

Infidelity is an act. It is not a thought. It is not a fantasy.

It is okay to dream, to look and to enjoy someone's company.

This is not a crime.

It is not infidelity.

It is natural and healthy to get validation from other people.

It is okay to lightly flirt with someone.

If your relationship's boundaries are too tight, you limit yourself and constrict the relationship.

You simply asphyxiate it!

The solution is to establish a higher level of trust.

Talk about it with your partner. Be light and open about it.

Accept these situations as part of life.

Remember: It is still with you she decides to be.

If you are in a committed relationship, there is a moral agreement between the two of you. Looking at another man does not break this moral agreement.

Give each other some space. It is healthy and truly beneficial for the relationship.

Give her the gift of your trust.

If you see her chatting with another man, you can as well express a positive form of jealousy. It is okay to claim your partner and show the world you two are together.

Do this if she is comfortable with it: go and kiss her in front of other men and send a clear message that she is not available.

This is a healthy type of action and is a "couple statement".

It is an affirmation of your mutual love.

Can you see how it works?

The key is always trust and complicity.

You know she is with you, even when she chats with another guy.

# She goes for after work drinks with her male colleagues

One key strategy: Do the same!

The moment you have your own set of female admirers, believe me, the whole power balance in your relationship shifts.

The reason you feel threatened by her going for drinks is because you feel left out.

Many guys hate their job and have zero opportunities for interesting social interaction within the work environment!

If she's having the time of her life, you might feel that it's simply not fair, right?

So! Boost your social connections and make sure that amongst them you have a couple of very attractive females.

This is REALLY THE ULTIMATE strategy in this situation.

Don't wait at home for her to come back and unload the details of her latest discussions with her male admirers.

Instead take proactive steps and start connecting with females fearlessly.

No shame! No guilt!

Remember that the key boundary in your relationship is probably: "No intimacy with someone else".

Having a chat with a female friend is NOT cheating.

It is chatting!

Chatting IS ok!

Never feel guilty for connecting with a woman, no matter how attractive she is.

This is the type of action that can actually trigger a whole chain reaction of interesting conversations with your girlfriend or wife.

For instance, if she hears about it and starts feeling slightly insecure or challenges you about it, here is what you can say:

YOU - "So, you think that I should not speak with other women than you???"

HER - "Well... She is obviously into you otherwise she would never have given you her number..."

YOU - "So, you believe that you meeting your male colleagues after work is different?

HER - "Absolutely! They are just friends..."

YOU - "So, if I was working with a VERY attractive female colleague and I was going with her for drinks after work, you would be ok with that?"

HER - "Well... I would need to be sure that you won't cheat on me!!! When a guy spends time with a woman there is ALWAYS potential for something more!"

YOU - "So, when you have a chat with a male colleague, there is always potential for more???"

GOT YOU!

You see? Right there, you just nailed it!

That's called reversing the situation.

You just made her understand EXACTLY how it feels to be in your shoes when she is at a bar having a drink with colleagues.

Now, you are not saying that she has to stop.

You are saying that:

- A few words of reassurance in your direction might help.
- She needs to understand the exact boundary between what is ok and what is not.

- If she does it, she needs to be able to take it the other way round as well.

My point is that the moment you decide to do the same, it forces her to look at her own patterns + come up with relationship boundaries that work well for both of you.

If you simply walk to her with a needy voice and ask her who these guys are, you will feel totally powerless in this conversation.

She will put you down and smother you with an "Oh... They are just friends... Do you feel threatened by that??"

You don't have to beg!

Take the step and simply practice the reverse strategy!

Meet your own set of female friends and observe carefully what happens next...

# She prefers chatting with her girlfriends

Girls can share lots of stuff she won't ever share with you.

They gossip and support each other.

That's THEIR gift.

You have a whole set of potentials with her and what she gets from you might be totally different than what she gets from her female friends.

That's ok, right?

It is still with you she is engaged in a romantic relationship.

Now, if you feel you lack emotional intimacy with her, that's something you can develop consciously.

The first step is for her to feel secure in your presence.

It is hard for her to trust you if what you bring to the table are usually problems and challenging issues.

She needs to be able to relax with you, so give her comfort and nurture harmony at all times.

Once you achieve that, become a good listener.

Women love sharing once they realize you actually enjoy hearing what she says.

The next step is to invite her to share more with follow up questions.

That's actually a coaching technique but it is definitely something you can ad to your conversation skills.

Say things like:

"Tell me more about that..."

"If I get you right, you are saying that..."

"So, what would you do if..."

These are all invitations to share.

Once she starts sharing, you need to be a good listener.

Creating emotional intimacy with your partner is a skill you can train.

It does ad a new dimension to your relationship.

What about her girlfriends, how should you stand in that?

Well... Let her know that you are happy for her having these friends.

Be ok when she has a night out with them.

Be friendly with these girls when they come for a visit.

You REALLY don't need to compete with them.

Having them ads actually value to her life and expands your network as a couple.

It is a good thing she has them in her life.

# Her work always comes first!

Another big potential source of disappointment for guys!

This is another area that can create lots of tension and you need a solid strategy to tackle that.

She can work as much as she wants!

That's her time!

That's her career!

She is free!

This is the general idea.

Trying to limit her or force her to spend time with you will achieve the exact opposite to what you want.

What you can do is openly invite her for things which are fun and let her make her own choices.

You can say things like:

"We'll be going out with Paul, his girlfriend and two other buddies to this new club... I heard it is pretty fantastic! I know you often need to stay late at work on Friday so, you are of course totally free to choose if you want to join us or not..."

You see, the moment you try to force her, she feels she has the right to defend herself.

If what you offer is simply an open invitation it is HER choice and HER responsibility to do what she wants with it.

If she feels she misses opportunities, than she can only blame herself.

The essential key in all this is that you must have a life beyond what you share with her.

If you are simply bored at home waiting for her to come back and entertain you, that's not too empowering, is it?

www.vitalcoaching.com

You need to activate your social life and build up connections where she is not involved.

This will give you a whole new social base and ad an extra refreshing edge to your relationship.

# She systematically chooses for her kids

If you are dating a single mother, this will happen and it is VERY natural!

Her kids are her life.

They will always come first!

They need her protection and love.

So, simply prepared!

If you date a single mother you will always come second after her kids.

Does this mean that such relationship can't work?

Of course not?

You still have lots of potential space and possibilities to connect deeply in a VERY fulfilling relationship.

Let's put it this way:

If you have your own business for instance and this venture needs your attention, you won't simply drop everything because she wants you to, right?

This is your life!

Her kids are hers and they were there before you met her.

You don't need to compete with them for attention.

I agree though... If all you get from her is a 2 hours date once a month, it might not be enough.

This is always a topic you can bring up carefully and let her know that if she had more time you would be happy to take her trekking or do more fun things together.

However, you must never pressure her!

If what you say sounds like demands, she will feel threatened and use her power to defend her family.

You can ask open ended questions like:

"How do you feel we could handle that?"

"How do you feel about this?"

"Spending more time together? Is this a wish you have or are you satisfied with what we share now?"

These open ended questions are a great way to open a conversation because they are not finger pointing.

There is no accusation. No one is being blamed.

We are simply exploring possibilities together.

Can you see how it works?

# Part 7 - Worried she will cheat? – Spying on her?

# Is there a way to make sure that she never cheats on you?

Being 100% protected from it? No, there isn't!

You can make sure though that the probabilities for her taking that step are very slim.

How do you do that?

- You make sure that she gets her needs met in your relationship.
- You are at your best and attractive!
- You have an open line of dialogue through which you communicate effectively.
- You keep your sex life exciting.
- She gets the attention she needs from you.
- You take time to be romantic, passionate and nurture your love life.
- You make plans for the future.
- You keep on evolving.
- You stay in good shape and take good care of yourself, your social life and career.
- Etc.

The key word here is "Attraction"!

The more she is attracted to you, the less she will want to meet someone else.

You stay attractive by expressing your power and confidence.

You keep your life interesting and moving forward!

The goal is not to lock her in! She does not want that anyway, right?

The goal is to create for yourself a life base she stays attracted to!

Big difference!

Now, here is what does not work or sends her away:

- Trying to control her activities and being over jealous and possessive. I am sure you guessed that one already! :)
- Asking her for endless emotional support.
- Expressing your insecurities to her and hoping she will solve them for you.
- Getting stacked in your life and stopping taking risks.
- Being enslaved by an addiction or self destructive behavior.
- Focusing your life too much on comfort and not enough on excitement.
- Failing to keep your sex life exciting!
- Etc!

There is much more of course.

Basically, if the relationship is good with you, she has no reason to go and look somewhere else.

Now a big mistake guys make is to believe that security is the most important factor.

You know... House, money, etc.

It's not! It counts only for 1/3 in the relationship's equation.

Thrill, excitement and fresh perspectives take as much space in her mind.

A fulfilling sex life is as well essential of course.

Guys often lose their girlfriend or wife because they are too soft or too kind.

If you want her to feel like a woman, you need to behave like a male!

Don't get mistaken! When she says that she wants you to share your feelings more, she is simply trying to establish a new refreshing communication line with you.

This kind of statement is actually very misleading and confusing for guys! If you do what she says and turn your relationship into an ongoing therapy circle, there are good chances that she will in fact be turned off!

One of these key couple mysteries we'll solve in another post!

For now remember that if you want her to feel feminine, you need to express your malehood!

Power and self confidence are the two key qualities you can focus on.

Uncontrolled jealousy outbursts are definitely not the type of power we are thinking of!

Uncontrolled jealousy is an expression of insecurity and emotional abuse!

It does not glorify you!

If actually makes you look weak because you become the slave of an emotion you don't control.

# She cheated before! - I am worried she will cheat again!

We are again in a situation where your jealousy is justified.

Something is definitely unsolved!

After your girlfriend cheated, you need to heal the open wounds.

You do that through dialogue and rebuilding the complicity between you and your girlfriend.

If she can't guarantee you that she won't cheat again, you have to shift the way you stand in your relationship and protect yourself.

How do you do that?

You take some emotional distance and gain back a new sense of independence.

As long as you are totally emotionally dependent on her, you will get hurt.

You can't control her life if what she wants is freedom.

You need to develop a mind set and attitude in which you know you would be okay with or without her.

If she can't guarantee a commitment on her side, this means that you need a serious back up plan in case she cheats again.

Some girls will never give you guarantees. In fact, even marriage is not a guarantee.

Now, when you have enough power, confidence and resilience, this gives you the tools to pull back what you invested in this relationship when she cheats on you.

This means as well that your income, place where you live and emotional balance must not depend on her. You need to fully own these aspects of your life.

This is why working together or having a house or children together when there is no serious commitment is quite a risk.

You need to protect yourself and be ready for anything!

# If she cheated before

This is one of the situations where jealousy is justified.

If she cheated before and you can't trust her anymore, find out where she stands with that.

You respond with jealousy which is simply lack of trust.

You realize you can't invest yourself in the relationship the way you would like to.

Obviously, cheating kills mutual trust.

It is different if she comes back and realizes she made a huge mistake, asks for forgiveness, etc.

If you partner cheated but honestly asks for forgiveness, there are some good chances you could get back together and have a healthy relationship in the future.

This "adventure" can even empower your relationship and establish a new level of mutual trust and complicity.

However, if you realize that she is not 100% committed to you and that cheating could happen again, you are trying to protect a very unstable territory.

It takes two strong pillars to preserve the relationship's space.

You can't do that alone.

She is not 100% committed? Fine, you can't force her.

The solution?

Step back as well.

Flirt with other women.

If she reacts, ask her if she is 100% committed to you and if she could be running away with another man any time soon.

Can you see the dynamics?

<u>Don't give your life to someone who does not give it back to you</u>.

If she is uncommitted and you are committed, it drains you.

It creates an emotional tension in your system. It is like a need or desire you can't fulfill.

You wait for her to take steps.

The solution?

Step back as well and recover part of what you invested in her.

<u>Take your freedom back</u>.

You need extra power and determination to do this, but it will definitely stop you from being jealous.

Your jealousy is related with the fact you have too high expectations.

She wants to keep her freedom?

Fine... Do the same.

# Should you check on her?

Suppose you have doubts.

You have the feeling she is not telling you the truth.

Should you take action and dare for instance to check her emails or follow her after work?

Is it okay to spy on your partner?

The answer is yes.

But you need to be very careful with what you do and why you do it.

95% of obsessive jealousy situations are unfounded.

In fact, jealousy is often delusional.

You imagine things that don't exist.

You interpret signs in an extreme way.

Basically, you distort reality.

Now, earlier I mentioned a few elements of what constitutes real cheating.

If you have doubts, it is effectively useful to check the facts and find out for yourself what the truth is.

Now, there are some very specific boundaries or limits you must respect.

Talk to her first!

Before you spy on your partner or do anything which invades her privacy, you must talk to her and ask her straight questions.

If you know that she is lying or get a feeling that something is wrong, I encourage you to take steps and check the facts.

Now, be very careful with how you interpret facts.

Finding a man's phone number in her time planner is not a proof of cheating; it is simply a proof that she is in contact with another man.

Now, this is not cheating.

It is not a crime.

Spying or other similar steps must be taken only as a last resort.

Spying is something which can happen once exceptionally.

If your intention is to set up hidden cameras in your partner's car for instance (just to be sure), this obviously crosses the line.

This is not a game. It is a last resort battle strategy aimed at defending your life and relationship.

It is better to verify doubts or feelings with real facts rather than letting them build up in your mind.

Get the answer and learn from it!

# Stop spying on her!

Some ways of spying are quite innocent.

Let's call this "level 1" spying.

In fact it is not even called spying.

It is called being curious.

In involves simple elements like recognizing the hand writing on the envelope of a letter she just received.

Another time, you might over hear a phone conversation she has with an ex simply because you happen to be there.

It happens because you are confronted with it. You were not really looking for it.

When you ask her where she has been, or what she did, it can be along the same line. This is sneakier and can be more invasive though.

You will say things like:

"I was worried about you!"

When in fact you were wondering with who she was and why she was not home at 6pm as usual.

This can become invasive if it is overdone and systematic of course.

The next level of spying (level 2) is when you actively take action to check what she's up to.

This involves checking her profile on a dating site to see if she has been active on it lately.

It is still non invasive to a point because you don't betray her privacy. Her profile is there for everyone to see.

In the next stage (level 3), you definitely cross the line:

- You check her cell phone records.

- You check her text messages.
- You enter her email account.
- You read her personal mail.
- You search her belongings looking for clues,
- Etc.

This one is a big No-No unless you have very good reasons to believe she is cheating on you.

It is an invasion of her privacy!

Realize that when you take that step, this could be a deal breaker for your relationship if she finds out about it.

There is one more level after that (level 4) which is following her, using detective tactics on her or hiring someone to do that!

The exact definition or model of these spying levels is not that important. I just made them up to make you realize that not all spying is the same.

Now, many men will indulge in a level 1 "spying-curiosity".

They ask questions. They are exposed to signs of her activities and who she is seeing.

That one is usually okay.

Now if you took any other step (level 2-4) or you aggressively ask her invasive questions about her activities over and over again, you probably start falling in the category of unwanted jealousy attitudes, right?

You want to get rid of that.

If you went to level 3 one time, thought she was cheating and found nothing, listen to that sign, forgive yourself and go back to the "I trust you" pattern.

Now, the best way to stop spying on her is to consciously drop it.

When you are tempted, you just sit down, wait for a minute and repeat to yourself:

"I am here to protect your freedom, not to limit you."

Depending on the intensity of your tendency to spy on her, it can easily take a month of focus to shift that behavior.

Even if you fall back, listen to the signs and what you found.

If she is not cheating, see it as a learning experience and use it to shift your behavior in the future.

If you found nothing, this usually means that your suspicions were ungrounded.

Spying on her is just another expression of your jealousy or insecurity. It is another way of expressing it.

Sometimes, you can express it verbally, other times you express it via this type of spying behaviors.

Ask yourself these questions:

What is the level, intensity and frequency of your spying/curiosity?

Does it bother either you or her?

This will tell you exactly how urgent it is for you to take action.

# Should you tell her that you have been spying on her?

Unless you found something and want to confront her, no!

It is not necessary!

You need to forgive yourself, realize that your suspicions were ungrounded and that you can in fact trust her.

When you spy on her, you take a risk!

If you feel guilty, you need to be able to live with your actions and forgive yourself.

Consider that you did what was right at that time. It was your best shot at defending your relationship and showing that you cared.

Learn from that experience and discover exactly why you will not do it again:

- You realized that your fears were delusional.
- You prefer trusting her.
- You did change and mature emotionally.
- You were vulnerable and found yourself back.
- Etc.

If your couple is strong and you know that telling her would not be an issue, it is okay to open up of course.

However, many women can't take this type of behavior!

It could destroy the trust she has in you!

If your priority is to protect your relationship, act accordingly and don't tell her anything she can't take, really.

If you think it was a mistake, it was yours, not hers!

Deal with it!

# Should you confront her if you know she is lying?

Yes! Definitely yes!

However you need to do it right.

First, you need proof that she is lying.

Maybe you spied on her and checked her email or cell phone.

This means that you have real proof, not just feelings.

If all you have are vague feelings, you can't confront her. It won't work.

Once you have gathered solid proofs, you need to realize as well that you spied on her.

She will accuse you of not trusting her.

The next step is to choose the right timing and attitude for that.

You don't want to point your finger at her and tell her how bad she is.

You want to sit down and have an open dialogue about what is going in your relationship.

My guess is that you still care and that you still want her.

If it is the case, the goal is to empower your relationship, not to find someone to blame.

Say something like: "I face a challenge with our relationship and I need your help to solve this dilemma. When is a good time to talk about this?"

If she accuses you of spying on her, you can say:

"Yes! We both did something which betrays the trust in our relationship. We are both guilty. Now, what are we going to do about it?"

If she says:

"First, I need you to promise me that you won't do that again..."

You can say:

"If I have serious reasons to believe that you are cheating on me, I will use any tool I can to find out what is truly going on."

"Now, my turn. You cheated on me. How do you feel about what happened?"

The best way to go is: no demand and no pressure.

# Part 8 - Your exes and female friends

# Why do I feel jealous when I see my ex with her new man?

Well, it's very simple!

You used to be together and when you were together you developed a natural desire to protect your relationship.

Jealousy is simply the expression of that desire to protect your relationship.

Whenever another guy would come closer to your girlfriend, you would wake up this emotional reaction which would sound like:

"It's with me she is. Stay away from her!"

Yes! This is jealousy!

And there is nothing wrong with expressing small dozes of it in your relationship as long as you don't become a slave of it.

Now, what happens when you break up?

You end a relationship but some of the emotional reactions associated with your ex stay in your mind.

You might feel desire for her, slightly possessive, or even imagine your future with her even though you rationally know that you are no longer together.

To stop the jealousy pattern, you need to consciously reprogram your mind and develop a new set of emotions when you are around her.

# Jealous of your ex partner's new relationship

When you break up with your partner, your ex will probably meet someone else.

This creates jealousy as well.

If this does not happen when you are around, it is probably easier to deal with it.

When you partner with someone, there is always some form of mutual control involved.

Jealousy is an expression of this control.

Control is a sustaining force for the relationship.

It is a power which keeps things together.

The moment you break up, you stop working on the relationship but some emotional patterns tend to survive the break up.

The moment you see your ex with someone else, you have a "claiming" reaction: "Hey! That's <u>my</u> woman"

You know it is not the truth but you still did not train your emotions to react in a different way.

<u>It is a left over conditioning</u>.

Being a bit jealous is okay as long as it does not consume you.

If it consumes you, it is the sign that you are still emotionally too invested in your ex.

What is the way to solve this reaction? <u>Let go!</u>

Consciously train your response:

"Hey, I am really happy for you. It is good that you and I can move on and stay friends. Can I introduce you to my new girl friend?"

You might "pretend" in the beginning.

You might struggle with negative emotions.

However, you can retrain this response if you want to:

- "She does not belong to me anymore"
- "She is free to do what she wants"
- "I am happy for you"
- etc.

Try it out. You'll see how it feels.

<u>The moment you let go of something you can't control, it is immensely liberating.</u>

It frees you from an inner tension.

You simply let go.

Empower the way you stand in this situation and consciously decide how you want to deal with it.

Find the emotional attitude, the inner posture you can take which does not hurt.

Find out how you can stand in it, so that you don't feel inner tension.

Think of yourself first.

This is about you!

This is about finding you inner balance.

How can you stand in this, so that you don't feel tension?

Find the right "mind posture".

# My ex is chatting it up with other guys on Facebook!

Another question that really strikes me!

The key word here is "Ex girlfriend".

This tells you straight away that a jealousy pattern is unjustified.

It does appear, sure! But it's an emotion which is totally useless and self destructive whether you act on it or not.

In other words; you don't want it, right?

You want to get rid of it! You want to go to battle so that the jealousy response disappears forever out of your mind.

Guess what? It is within your range to actually achieve just that!

What about the anger?

Well, anger is a different story!

Why? Because anger is actually here to serve you.

Let's dive into it...

Anger is a fire or power trying to break free in your system.

Anger is actually the reflection of a freeing force breaking through your body and mind.

Imagine a volcano ready to explode because this lava or inner power is being constricted.

When you break up you need to free yourself from your ex.

Anger is the awakening of this inner freeing fire. In other terms anger is okay! It is actually good and natural and trying to suppress it will be counterproductive.

Now, you are not allowed to act on it or hurt anyone with this anger. You need to find other ways of channeling it until your system "digests" it.

The best is to go to the gym and do some power training. You can do that outdoor as well. You can focus on your career or launch a new business.

All these are creative expressions of your anger.

Remember!!!! You are not allowed to hurt yourself or anyone else, so don't even think about it!

See anger as a creative fire which has the power to open new doors in your life.

It destroys the past and creates new space for a new future to be born.

Without this inner fire you would stay stacked in old patterns you no longer want.

# Jealous when your friend with benefits finds another man?

Friend with benefits means that you are not committed, right?

That's the deal.

If you both agreed that dating other people was okay, there is nothing you can do but accept that that she does whatever she wants.

Now, being in this type of open relationship or love triangle situations is extra challenging.

Most people can't and don't want to take it.

This is why they decide to go for a committed relationship instead.

Now, if it's a situation you want to maintain with this girlfriend, here are a couple of ideas you can strengthen.

Any time you feel jealousy coming to the surface, reason yourself and go back to ideas like:

"She is free"

"She does what she wants"

"I have no right to tell her what to do!"

"This is what we agreed in the first place"

That's the first step. You need to create a new mind set and emotional reactions for the exact challenge you face.

This implies reconditioning (don't be scared! It's a good thing) yourself to respond differently.

# Female friend spends all her time with her new partner!

It's already tough to deal with jealousy issues when you are in a committed relationship!

Now, when you are friends, even best friends with someone, there is no commitment!

How can you claim someone who does not belong to you?!!!

In that situation, jealousy is an absolute waste of your time and energy!

It is destructive and frustrating for all those involved.

Get rid of that pattern and learn to be happy for her.

# **Conclusion**

I hope you enjoyed this material!

Feed back? Questions? Success stories?

Email me at francisco@vitalcoaching.com

For instant live help:

http://vitalcoaching.com/coaching.htm

For more topics on dating and personal power go to:

http://vitalcoaching.com

To your power

Francisco Bujan

Made in the USA
Middletown, DE
08 September 2023